THE AUTHENTIC LEADER AS SERVANT (ALS)

ALS I COURSE 10
TRUST – INTEGRITY LEADERSHIP
Attributes, Principles, and

SYLVANUS N. WOSU, Ph.D

THE AUTHENTIC LEADER AS SERVANT
ALS I COURSE 10
Developing Trust-Integrity Leadership Attributes, Principles, and Practices

© Copyright 2024 by Sylvanus N. Wosu Ph.D.

Printed in the United States of America
ISBN: 979-8-9858816-7-7

All rights reserved. No part of this book may be reproduced or transmitted in any form or by any means, electronic or mechanical, including photocopying, recording, or by any information storage and retrieval system, without permission in writing from the copyright owner.

Bible quotations are from the New King James (NKJV) version of the Bible unless otherwise indicated.

Other versions used in this book are the New International Version (NIV), New Living Translation (NLT), King James Version (KJV), English Standard Version (ESV), and Good News Translation (GNT). Unless otherwise specified, NKJV should be assumed.

The views expressed in this work are solely those of the author and do not necessarily reflect the views of the publisher, and the publisher disclaims any responsibility for them.

To order additional copies of this book, contact:
Proisle Publishing Services LLC
39-67 58th Street, 1st floor
Woodside, NY 11377, USA
Phone: (+1 646-480-0129)
info@proislepublishing.com

TABLE OF CONTENTS

FOREWORD	XI
ACKNOWLEDGMENTS	XV
DEDICATION	XIX
PREFACE	21
About Leader As Servant Leadership (LSL) Model	24
About the Authentic Leader as Servant (ALS)	27
About the ALS Courses	28

CHAPTER 1
UNDERSTANDING LEADERSHIP ATTRIBUTES — 37

- Functional Definitions — 37
- Comparisons With Other Works — 42
- Principle of Leadership Attribute — 44
- Authentic Leadership Attributes — 45
- Summary 1 Understanding Leadership Process — 50

CHAPTER 2
LEADERSHIP TRUST-INTEGRITY ATTRIBUTE — 53

- Characteristics of Trust Attribute — 54
- Principle of Leadership Trust Attribute — 56
- Summary 2 Leadership Trust-Integrity Attribute — 58

CHAPTER 3
DEVELOPING TRUST-CHARACTER — 61

- Summary 3 Developing the Act of Trust-Character — 64

CHAPTER 4
BUILDING TRUST-COMPETENCE — 67

- Summary 4 Developing the Acts of Trust-Competence — 69

CHAPTER 5
DEVELOPING THE ACTS OF TRUST-INTEGRITY — 73

- Summary 5 Developing Acts of Trust-Integrity — 79

CHAPTER 6
DISPLAYING TRUST-CREDIBLITY — 83

- Servant Leadership Transformative Principles — 85
- A Case of Credibility: David after God's Heart — 97

ALS TRUST-INTEGRITY LEADERSHIP
ATTRIBUTES, PRINCIPLES, & PRACTICES

Summary 6 Developing the Acts of Trust-Credibility -------------------------- 100

TOPIC INDEX 105
REFERENCES 107

FOREWORD

The modern world today is obsessed with standardization and modalities. As a result, in the realm of leadership, many books have spout associated leadership theories and models and explain them as the path to follow. However, the critical dimensions that distinguish the effectiveness of any leadership process are the values and attribute the leader brings to the table; desired change is influenced by leadership styles or standards. These many standards and theories of leadership often are not in step with the changing times or the followers' needs. The trend is a bit like stocking different kinds of foods in a grocery store and expecting that they will meet everybody's needs the same way and at all times. Aisles are packed with varieties of food with expiration dates in the future, but getting the best deal on the products is what really matters to those who buy and use the products

In many ways, this is the state of leadership in the modern world. Increasingly, even leaders of public institutions are tasked with turning a profit for themselves or the organization they serve. The idea of a "leader" seems to float uneasily alongside the ranks of fundraisers or profit raisers in contrast to any kind of role model for followers or employees. That which is knowable, measurable, and marketable has surpassed the difficult intangibility of strong moral leadership attributes as the central guideline for achievement and success.

In this complicated space, Dr. Sylvanus Wosu introduces his complex idea of the Leader as a Servant Leadership, which is in this book, modeled on Christian tradition. Like all intricate ideas, Dr. Wosu's central point depends on a paradox: a person is best qualified to lead when he or she is most ready to serve. This paradox has been monopolized rhetorically by "public servants" who often serve either self-interest or the interests of specific lobbies. The Authentic Leader as Servant penetrates past the superficial concept of "serving" and details the internal state of true servitude or Servanthood.

While the book is primarily focused on the Christian model of leadership attributes such as discipleship, empathy, affection, and Servanthood, it does so not merely on the grounds of blind faith, but rather via numerous contemporary sociological and business-driven studies on how leaders should seek a leader-follower relationship that is simultaneously productive and nurturing. Dr. Wosu's most piercing insights always involve this secular–Christian dialogue. This book demonstrates that Christ's model for leadership is one that may exist successfully outside the confines of a faith relationship; it places the values of Christ's religious significance in leadership at the center of the framework. It is clear from Dr. Wosu's generous own life story of faith—a faith tested by humbling difficulties—is at the center of both his orientation and motivation for writing.

In language that is so concise, it is often illustrated in mathematical formulas; Dr. Wosu explains the deep structural integrity of Christ's Leader as the Servant Leadership model. One could imagine leaders of any doctrine benefiting from the analyses contained in these pages. The book's message repeatedly encourages the reader to imagine a scenario or reflect on memories and personal experiences to prove or test its many points. Thus, the book depends on a form of praxis, a lesson that could be or has been enacted, by the participating reader. I am very impressed at the volume and level of thinking of the author. Parts of the book involve his personal story, which is especially riveting. I cannot imagine what he had to endure, which he referred to as a" wilderness walk," to accomplish the goal he set for himself. His life stories on these pages are inspiring and stimulating.

In this way, the text eschews dogmatism in favor of the self-discovery Socratic Method of teaching and learning. The reader is not badgered into complying with a religious objective but is rather asked to consider the applicability of difficult biblical concepts in relation to modern life. It is a fascinating and very thought-provoking read.

Hence, the book does not seek to make the leader a servant, a cookie-cutter corporate buzzword, but rather asks the reader to imagine him or herself interacting with a range of concepts. One of Dr. Wosu's great strengths is his reservation when it comes to forcing his reading's interpretation on the material he presents.

The book parallels Biblical and modern leadership scenarios in ways that consistently provoke thought, and while it is clear Dr. Wosu has his particular leadership style; the space for the reader's own thoughts is always left open.

The book could not have been written in any other way with integrity. Its format and formulas are offered to the reader of the leader as a servant role that it analyzes in its pages. To find a text that instructs from this humble position is profoundly refreshing in a genre that is often packaged inside a cover with a sizeable picture of the "modest" author, smiling egotistically beneath a name spelled out in large, gold lettering. Throughout its pages, this text feels as if it serves the reader.

In the end, this is the most satisfying aspect of the book. There is no standardized approach to achieving successful leadership. There is no promise of power and a bigger payday; in fact, the book often proffers just the opposite. The reader is not encouraged to devalue the experience of leadership by finding some economic metric for marking success but is rather asked to think deeply about the most basic elements of internal and social interaction within the framework of a Christian tradition. What this means will be different for every reader. Indeed, even in the context of single chapters, I found myself questioning or re-evaluating moments of my own life. This book serves; it doesn't feel like filling in multiple-choice questions, staring at a wall of flavorless grocery products, or hearing the endless servant promises of today's political scene. It feels like a humble invitation to consider a single paradoxical element of a profoundly productive tradition.

-Tobias Bates

Acknowledgments

A book on leadership attributes as aspects of Servant Leadership sprouted from the wealth of knowledge and the inspirations of many other leaders. Their writings were sources of inspiration, challenges, and examples of excellence to emulate. I acknowledge the leaders listed below for their help in one way or the other. I am very grateful and I hereby express my appreciation and thanks:

Mr. Wayne Holt, introduced me first to the subject of Servanthood in one of our Stephen Ministerial Training classes, and he is the one who has conducted his life as a leader–servant; he encouraged me throughout my writing;

Dr. Harvey Borovetz, Distinguished Professor and Chair of the Bioengineering Department, is a leader-servant in many ways, he modeled Servanthood and encouragement attributes throughout his leadership in an academic setting.

Dr. Clifford and Dr. Patience Obih, in so many measures exemplified the practical leadership attributes discussed in this book.

Pastor Lance Lecocq, Lead Pastor of Monroeville Assembly of God, for his excellent model of servanthood, empowerment, and emulation attributes to the ministerial team, I am thankful for his motivation and encouragement throughout the several hours on this project;

To my administrative assistant, Ms. Terri Cook, who was always the first to review the manuscript; I am very grateful for her dedication.

To the African Christian Fellowship USA, institutions, and all other organizations where I have served in one leadership capacity or the other, thank you for affording me senior leadership positions that provided the leadership platform and opportunities to grow as a leader.

Dr. Lawrence Owoputi, a brother I am proud to call my friend; for his dedication to serving others, his generosity, healing care, and responsibility attributes during our term in office and in chapter leadership positions; he taught me that excellent following is also part of good leadership;

To Tobias Bates, for his editorial work on the original draft of the book, and his dedication to completing the work.

Mr. Edward F. Kondis, a member of our Engineering Board of Visitors, for his always encouraging and moral support;

Dr. Enefaa N. Wosu, my wife and life partner, for her love, commitment, and prayer support, especially during those long night hours I was not there for her and her constant reminder of who I must be as a leader-servant. Without her support, forbearance, wisdom, and encouragement, this project would not have been completed; I say, thank you very much.

And to God alone be all the glory and honor for the divine inspiration and guidance in initiating and completing this life-transforming book project.

DEDICATION

I humbly submit this book back unto the gracious hands of God who inspired the writings through His Holy Spirit!

I dedicate this book to my virtuous wife of 45 years, Rev. (Dr.) Enefaa Wosu whose spiritual leadership is an important gateway to our home, and to our four wonderful children—Prof. Eliada Wosu-Griffin EL, HeCareth, Tamuno-Emi, and Chidinma. From them all, I learnt what it meant to be a leader-servant. I could not be blessed with better teachers.

PREFACE

What characteristics did Biblical leaders like the Apostle Paul, Moses, Joshua, and Nehemiah as servants of their people display outwardly that distinguished them from other leaders, both then and now? The Apostle Paul kept his focus to *emulate* Christ and endured all the infirmities and persecutions he suffered to complete his goal to preach the gospel of Jesus Christ. He inspired Timothy and others through his effective *discipleship* leadership to imitate him as he emulated Christ. Moses' outward display of his *trust* in God's power earned him a good level of trust from the people and empowered him for the mission of delivery of God's children from bondage in Egypt; he had to *reproduce* himself in Joshua to complete the mission. But the greatest of them was Jesus Christ, who humbly sacrificed His life to finish the work of redemption. In His *Servanthood*, commitment, and love for the people, He became the ultimate *model* of a leader as a servant to *emulate*.

Let's consider for a moment secular leaders in these current times! For example, think of Henry Ford, who founded the successful Ford Motor Company; Bill Gates who created the global empire that is Microsoft; Albert Einstein, who in many ways is synonymous with a genius for his contributions to modern physics; Abraham Lincoln, remembered as one of the greatest presidents and leaders of United States; and many others like these we cannot mention. What did all these leaders have in common? What propelled them to turn their initial failures or challenges into eventual successes? None had a direct mentor or inherited any fortune from their parents. Nevertheless, they all eventually succeeded. These people can be distinguished from others based on their self-will to succeed, their self-confidence and belief in themselves, their self-determination, and their perseverance, among other characteristics. The distinguishing characteristics displayed externally in service or relationships toward others are the outward functional attributes that define that leader.

Think about yourself as a student, faculty member, or that new executive. What was it that made your journey to success different and even great? Students and colleagues, when they see or hear about my display of what I have referred to as the 'wilderness walk of faith', have asked me to share the critical attitudinal elements that made me remain inwardly resilient and undaunted and yet outwardly joyful in the difficulties I had faced. This book is the result of those reflections. Let me explain one such teaching moment.

Many years ago, sitting in my research lab on a Saturday morning trying to finish writing my dissertation, a fellow graduate student walked into the room to talk with me. He was contemplating terminating his graduate studies. He was a privileged single male student but felt the load was just too much.

"Sylvanus," he asked, with seriousness in his eyes, "your research advisor suggested that I should ask you, 'what is it that makes you tick?'.'What is it about you that makes you joyful and at peace with yourself and determined to finish, no matter the situations and high expectations we face in this department?"

What he asked me were deeply reflective questions, but I was willing and excited to answer them. Even so, before I do, let's look at the context. At that period in my life, I had four little children as a graduate student; in fact, more children than any of the faculties at that time, except for one faculty member who had eight children. I received little or no support from the department. I was then an international alien, did not qualify for financial aid, and was not given any research assistant position. I was, therefore, self-supported with two off-campus part-time jobs. I joked at being a minority of minorities, the only student in the department with such a label,—but I was self-willed to succeed. My adaptability attribute, coupled with perseverance and resilience, was all that I needed to succeed despite the odds against me. In every exam, homework assignment, or project I had to compete with students with full financial aid, plus they had nothing to distract their attention from their studies. I lived with the attitude that using disadvantages as an excuse was not an option. Aspiring to earn my Ph.D. was a life dream, and I was willing to give my ultimate best to actualize that dream even in the face of challenges. The choice was mine!

So I looked at my classmate and all I could see was a student striding through a valley through which I also walked. He needed me to show him how to walk the walk, to empathize with him. To answer his question, I smiled, not that I wanted to, but because it was just who I was. The joy he attributed to me was an overflow of my appreciation of God's grace that His life in me was externally manifesting His light to bless someone else. It was a great teaching moment; I capitalized on it to tell my classmate that my joy was not about me. He could see physically but about He who was in me, he could not see in the flesh; I needed him to know that I was just showing forth His life in me. At first, my classmate did not understand the spiritual prose or metaphor I was using. He looked surprised but open to hearing more.

I did not ask if he was a Christian. However, right on my desk was my small green pocket Bible. I opened to 2 Corinthians 12:9 (NIV) and handed it to him to read. As he read the passage: "But he said to me, 'My grace is sufficient for you, for my power is made perfect in weakness.' Therefore, I will boast all the more gladly about my weaknesses, so that Christ's power may rest on me," I noticed how absorbed he was in the words

He looked astonished and read it again, this time silently. "This is interesting, but what does this mean?" He asked. I took his question to mean, "How does this relate to my question?

I explained to my friend that the external attitudes he or my advisors saw in me that warranted the question, "What makes you tick" were inspired by my inner value system based on my faith in this same Christ and His teachings. My desire to manifest His life and self-confidence is all because of what He has promised in His word if I believed. I have believed His words and have gained self-determination and faith to make the right choices through Him for my life, and his spirit has given me perseverance and resilience to focus on finishing strong in pursuit of any goal. "With that faith, I have continued, more passionately and excitedly; I can look at my challenges and vulnerabilities and delight joyfully in them, even as an alien minority of minorities! His grace and power have empowered me to do all things I want to do. That is what makes me tick," I explained.

He looked at me as if he got his answer. "Wow, thanks!" he said, looking inspired and ready to face his challenges. As we concluded with a prayer, and he stood up to leave, I pointed empathetically to his face and said, "If I made it despite my challenges, you have absolutely no excuse but to persevere to complete your studies; you can make it too!"

It is fitting to report that this encounter with my classmate transformed his will and determination to continue. Yes, he was encouraged and went on to complete his graduate studies. He emulated self-will and perseverance from the example of the most vulnerable of all students in the department.

The inner value system of a Leader-Servant is founded not only on his faith but his self-will, coupled with self-leadership; it is the greatest mentor who can turn any situation into an inconceivable success. Self-will is the primary driver for determination, resilience, and perseverance. It is what wakes you up in the morning to ask for strength to do whatever it is you are setting out to do. Based on my life walk of faith, I can state with absolute certainty that faith is the unseen assuredness that can empower you to turn your life's probable impossibilities into great and improbable possibilities.

ABOUT LEADER AS SERVANT LEADERSHIP (LSL) MODEL

Looking at the testimony above, do you know the source that energizes the characteristics you display outside and how your inner self is related to what others see outside? What distinguishes you from others is what combines to define your attributes! As a follower, can you identify the characteristics that distinguish your leaders? As an executive, how do you base your evaluation of yourself? Or how do you evaluate that brand-new manager or new youth director you want to hire? To what do you compare the individual's qualities when you look at his CV? What is the basis of your measure? Do you know if you are a substantial leader? These personal questions and much more are the subjects of this two-volume book, 'The Authentic Leader as Servant Part I: The Outward Leadership Attributes, Principles, and Practices', is written in two parts; the second part 'The Leader as Servant Leadership Model. Part II'; deals with the Inner Strength Leadership Attributes, Principles, and Practices.

When we think about today's corporate greed, deepening divide between the haves and have-not, gridlock in political systems, conflicts and wars, high divorce rates, and the rich young ruler in the Bible, it is easy to agree that all these people share a few things in common: self-centeredness, pride, lack of compassion, and greed. There is a great need in today's suffering world for leader-servants who display leadership attributes. These attributes should be oriented toward selfless service to others. Indeed, our world is increasingly drifting away from global serving reality toward the self and apathy. The most credible message or model for a possible solution to this dilemma and the answer to several complex leadership questions can be found in the foundation of the ultimate leader-servant, Jesus Christ. This book defines the Leader as Servant Leadership attribute as the combined acts of two or more distinctive functional leadership characteristics exhibited in service and relationship toward others. There is no better time than now for a book that presents comprehensive and irrevocable facts and principles regarding how to develop effective attributes of the leader-servant.

The Leader as Servant Leadership Model

My first book on this subject, The Leader as Servant Leadership Model, explains that Jesus' servant leadership model is based on the notion of a Leader as a Servant and not on a Servant as Leader. There are four distinct differences between a Servant as Leader (Servant-leader) and the Leader as Servant (leader--servant) models. It is pertinent to highlight them here to connect to this book, Authentic Leader as Servant.

A Leader as Servant is a leader first. The leader–servant as a leader does not in the line of duty go projecting or lording his or her power and authority over others but is the person to lead the process of influencing desired changes in others through his humble example of being a servant or having a serviceable attitude toward others. He or she is a serving leader, not a lording leader. He leads as a servant by putting others' needs above his own needs and rights. Jesus emphasized the word "as" meaning that the leader (the Master) chooses to serve as a servant even though he is the leader. A leader–servant emulates Jesus, who gave up all rights, and emptied and expended Himself on His followers. He empowered them to become more like Him. A leader-servant is known as a leader first but is seen as a great leader by his humble attendant heart and acts of service to others. His greatness comes from his ability to put others above himself.

Leader as Servant is a Biblical Concept. The model or image of a humble serving leader motivated Jesus' disciples to see that if their master could do this for them, they must also be able to do it for others. Jesus clearly demonstrated the process of leader-as-servant leadership. In some cases, He chose to serve by leading when He wanted to create the image or model of the leader-servant in certain acts. In other cases, He chose to lead by serving, when he showed care and empathy toward the people and led the disciples to see empathy as a leadership attribute.

Leader as Servant is an Authentic Leadership Model to follow. The Leader as the Servant leadership model intentionally positions Jesus as an original model of a leader to follow.

He was serving His disciples to demonstrate that the process of becoming a great leader was earned through humble acts of service to others; He made them understand that He was empowering them to succeed Him as leader-servants through service to others. The result was an incomparable legacy of leadership that changed their communities. The fact that Jesus relinquished his rights or shared His power did not diminish His power and influence. In fact, his influence increased at least 11 X 100%, if we ignore the one case of Judas.

The Leader as Servant Transforms Organizational Culture. The proposed LSL model seeks to transform and sustain the community or organization by instilling key leadership values or "leadership presence" among followers or an organization's members. Change is sustained when everyone in the organization takes ownership of the change. Rather than focusing on leading more followers to be great followers who conform to the organizational culture, LSL seeks to lead and empower better leaders to be distinguished leaders and community builders.

There are four distinctions, which clearly differentiate many of the existing servants as Leader-based philosophies in relation to servant leadership from my LSL model. Even in the corporate or institutional worlds, there is nothing better than Jesus on which to base Servant Leadership. There is nothing more authentic and impacting than the servant leadership modeled by the life and teachings of Jesus Christ.

The LSL model uses exploratory questions, scenarios, and graphic visualizations to excite critical thinking in ways no other book on this subject has yet attempted. Several personal testimonies of my wilderness walk of faith with God are used to connect the reader to real-life experiences of the concepts discussed. The riveting effect is that the text engages and encourages the reader to walk through the experiences presented. The aim is to inspire the reader spiritually, mentally, and professionally with this far-reaching exposition on the subject of servant leadership.

ABOUT THE AUTHENTIC LEADER AS SERVANT (ALS)

The *Authentic Leader as Servant* argues that no leadership model is as authentic, other-centered, able to build communities, and productive and service-oriented as the model of our ultimate leader-servant, Jesus Christ. No source can provide a better point of reference than that provided in the Bible. Hence, this book aims to be more than just a text on leadership; it hopes to be a personal discovery for those who aspire to develop effective leadership attributes that grow leaders as servants who ultimately develop thriving other-centered communities. This book presents a comprehensive, biblically-based study regarding how to develop these attributes and how they are applied in a servant leadership process. In this biblical context and for clarity, Servant Leadership means *Leader-as-Servant Leadership*. A *leader-servant* refers to a *leader as a servant*, which is distinct from a servant-leader or servant as leader.

Leader as Servant Leadership attributes are shaped by the Leadership's Inner Value system, which consists of character, motivation, and commitment. The *Authentic Leader as Servant* is presented as a necessary resource to complement my *The Leader as Servant Leadership (LSL) Model*. The LSL model integrates a transformative leadership framework and interactive dimensions of Servant Leadership. Leader as Servant Leadership is a process in which a leader, in his leadership position, purposefully chooses to put others' rights and needs above his positional rights and personal needs. He then serves, enables, and empowers followers for growth that builds a thriving organization. The LSL model looks at the predominant Servant Leadership concepts and shares how they compare with biblical principles on how we should lead and be led.

ABOUT THE ALS COURSES

The three books, *LSL Model* and *The Authentic Leader as Servant* (Parts I and II), together demonstrate that with today's global visions to reach people of all races and cultures, now is the time for an authentic servant's heart of service. Those visions and the leadership processes are most effective with the appropriate leadership attributes centered more on people than on the organization, principles regarding how to develop effective attributes of leader-servant.

The ALS I and II combined presented twenty leaders as servant leadership attributes. The series of ALS courses supply training guide to understand, develop, and practice the attributes in a leadership process. Each course is independent and self-contained and does not depend on completing any other course in the series of 20 courses. It is, however strongly recommended, in fact a must read, that chapters 1 and 2 in each series be covered as they lay the foundation of LSL model on which ALS is based.

ALS (Parts I & II) Course Layout

The *Authentic Leader as Servant (ALS)* leadership (parts I and II) book has been broken down into 20 courses in workbook format to achieve three goals 1) Self-discovery of the acts of developing the attribute under review in the course, 2) deeper understanding of the principles, research and biblical teaching behind the attributes, and 3) Learning the strategies for practicing the attributes.

Instruction

The set of questions following each chapter are designed to serve as a guide to discover, explore, and practice the essential ALS leadership attributes, principles, and practices in leadership process. The questions are comprehensive review based on the content of this specific chapter only.

To maximize the learning outcomes, the learner must read through this chapter and sections. Some referenced scriptures in the book are repeated in the summaries for added review if needed, even though they were discussed in the section in which they apply.

> The exercises that follow each chapter will help you in not only understanding your own strength and weaknesses in your acts of the attribute but will guide you in developing practical strategies you can apply in self-leadership process or helping others grow in leadership
>
> All answers to the questions are contained in the associated chapter or sections; consultation of new sources, except for the reference scriptures, is not needed. Thus, it is expected that you answer the questions after you have read the associated section or chapter of the workbook. The scripture or other references cited are only for references as they already discussed in the book

---

ALS I Course 1: Affection Leadership Attribute—*Affection flows from a person to produce positive emotions for the well-being of another person.*

An average person will define the word "love" in the sense that affection is a characteristic of love. Nevertheless, that definition clouds the functional meaning of affection as an attribute of a leader-servant. Affection is a love action intentionally given to someone to create favorable emotion. We experience a positive emotion when we receive or give affection. In his acts of affection, the Apostle Paul communicated to the Corinthian Christians how he spoke to them freely with an open heart, because it was an important way to give affection (2 Corinthians 6:11-13). He also spoke of longing for them with the affection of Jesus Christ (Philippians 1:8); an affection that needs to be mutual (1 Peter 1:7). How is the affection leadership attribute an outward leadership attribute? This course explores this and other questions to discover the characteristics of affection attributes and to formulate a functional principle based on the expected outcome of affection and the effective use of these attributes in leadership.

ALS I Course 2: Discipleship Leadership Attribute- *Discipleship transforms and empowers followers for service leadership that grows communities.*

Discipleship as an act of developing a follower toward a specific goal is an important function of leadership to equip others to lead. *Discipleship transforms and empowers followers for service leadership that grows communities*. A disciple is a follower who willingly chooses to follow the master and submits to his discipleship and authority. In that regard, Jesus wanted all his followers to be his disciples and ambassadors because a disciple is always a follower. Organizationally, a follower could be a junior employee, any employee in a brand-new department, a new younger faculty, or just any person that needs to be guided through a journey of professional growth and good success. This course focuses on the general growth of followers through the acts of discipleship and presents the critical characteristics of discipleship as a leadership outward attribute. Functional definitions of leadership discipleship attributes and its principle will be presented based on those characteristics. Each characteristic will be discussed in detail with emphasis on strategies of how they can be further developed or practiced as a part of the servant leadership process.

ALS I Course 3: Emulation Leadership Attribute—*A great leader-servant outwardly and positively inspires a pattern of good works for others to follow.*

To emulate is to strive to be like someone else or to follow someone else's example by imitating something that inspires you about that person. This course evaluates how to learn from someone good leadership qualities to develop yours. How did you use what you learned from following the footstep of your hero to grow your leadership qualities. Jesus in the scripture modeled humility and Servanthood he wanted his disciples to develop same qualities. Emulation as a leadership attribute shares some characteristics with transformative leadership, where a leader intentionally conveys a clear vision of a goal, inspires the passion for the work toward the goal, and motivates the followers to follow. As a leader, how do you model a characteristic behavior for someone to follow or develop? How is Leadership Emulation Leadership Attribute an outward leadership attribute? This course explores this and other questions to discover the characteristics of affection attributes and to formulate a functional principle based on the expected outcome of effective use of these attributes in leadership.

ALS I Course 4: Generosity Leadership Attribute: *Generosity is an outward measure of the level of sacrifice, what is shared, or the impact a giving makes, not just the size of the giving*

Generosity can be defined as "the *habit of giving* without expecting anything in return. It can involve offering time, assets, or talents to aid someone in need." Such habits can include spending your personal money, time, and/or labor for the welfare of others or expending (suffering or being consumed or spending) for others' well-being. When political leaders or Board members 'vote their conscience' on important issues that affect others, what is that "conscience" and how do such leaders contribute to the welfare of others? How can you, "Do all you can, with what you have, in the time you have, in the place where you are" for the betterment of humanity All giving to help humanity is crucial to help meet the needs of the most vulnerable of God's children, as demonstrated by God as attribute of God, In this course, we will explore what distinguishes a leader's act of giving from his inside intentions. The key leadership characteristics of generosity will be discussed with respect to Servant-Leadership generosity Attributes and Principles and the details how a leader-servant can develop those characteristics and then effectively practice service leadership.

ALS I Course 5: Healing-Care Leadership Attribute: *Comforting others in any trouble with the comfort with which God comforts us, brings healing-wholeness*

What is healing Care and what does it mean in practical terms to you as a leader? Effective leadership begins with an emotionally and spiritually healthy leader who can reconcile and bring comfort to the followers, irrespective of followers' feelings (good or bad) toward the leader. The healing attribute and personal security complement each other. You must have the capacity for self-healing and individual security if you are to meet others' comforts. Personal security provides the infrastructure to support leaders in adversity and heal others that are hurting. A leader's or a group's success is measured by the strength of the weakest member or follower in the group or team… Healing is one of the most abstract and least understood attributes in leadership, and yet one of the most important. The key distinguishing characteristics will be explored to formulate a working definition and principle of leadership healing-care attributes based on those characteristics. Each characteristic will be discussed in detail with emphasis on strategies of how they can be further developed or practiced by a leader-servant as part of the servant leadership process.

ALS I Course 6: Influence Leadership Attribute-*The true measure of leadership success in affecting desired change in conduct, performance, and relational connections in others is influence*

Leadership is an integrative process in which a person applies appropriate (leadership) attributes to guide and influence the desired attitudinal changes in others toward accomplishing a particular goal. Eight five percent of CEOs of top companies surveyed on their climb to leadership ladder said they were "influenced by another leader," compared to 10% and 5% for "natural gifting" and "result of a crisis," respectively. When we consider influence as a servant leadership attribute, we are talking about a distinguishing leadership characteristic that displays on the outside what a leader is inside, influence takes on a deeper meaning. In this course, the key leadership characteristics of influence will be identified and explored from research to frame definitions of the Servant-Leadership influence attribute and principle. Based on those characteristics, the key outcomes of effective leadership influence l how a leader-servant can develop those characteristics and then effectively practice service leadership.

ALS I Course 7: Persuasion Leadership Attribute—*The means of transforming others to a new perspective is through empathetic persuasion.*

Persuasion attribute affords the leader the capacity to convince his followers or others to believe and engage in a new idea or goal through encouragement rather than using his positional authority or intimidation. Because members of the group may already have their views on an issue, the leader must carefully approach persuasion as a learning process to avoid conflicts or polarizing the group. He must unify the diversity of views to get buy-in and willingness to agree and follow. The leader-servant primarily relies on making decisions within an organization based on persuasion rather than positional authority. In other words, you will never hear the Leader-servant say, "Do it because I am the boss, and I say to." This particular element offers one of the clearest distinctions between the traditional authoritarian model of leadership and the concept of Servant leadership. In this course, we will explore the technique of convincing rather than coercing as one of the most effective ways a leader-servant can build consensus within groups. Key characteristics of persuasion leadership attribute will be found, fully discussed, and modeled from the examples in the lives of other leaders.

ALS I Course 8: Reproduction Leadership Attribute—*Great leaders produce successors for legacy and greater courses as an expected product of an effective leadership reproduction.*

In his book, *360 Degree Leader*, John C. Maxwell says, "Great leaders don't use people so they can win. They lead people so they can all lead together." Such great leaders, like Jesus, Moses, Paul, and others developed other leaders through a process of reproduction. Is it possible for leaders of today to reproduce their vision in others so that can lead and build a legacy together? The answer to this question is of course yes. However, the effectiveness of a leader duplicating his leadership qualities in a follower depends on the leadership reproduction attribute of the leader. This course explores the distinguishing characteristics of reproduction as an outward attribute in servant leadership. Functional definitions of leadership reproduction attribute and its principle will be presented based on those characteristics. Each characteristic of reproduction attributes will be discussed in detail with emphasis on strategies of how they can be further developed or practiced by a leader-servant as part of the servant leadership process.

ALS I Course 9: Servanthood Leadership Attribute— *A leader-servant is most qualified to lead when ready to serve as a servant for the growth of others.*

The last time you engaged in a practical act of service on the job, at home, church, or in your community, what were the key elements in that act of service? Did you serve because you wanted to and chose to serve? Or was it because someone asked you to? The ultimate goal is for the leader's life to positively transform many lives in his or her community of followers. Consider the New Testament teachings of Jesus, who demonstrated the ultimate Leader as Servant Leadership. Jesus equated greatness to serving unpretentiously (humbly, as would a child), and He equated leading with choosing to serve others. That is the first affirmative test of authenticity for this attribute. What were the distinguishing characteristics that enabled you to serve? How is the Leadership Servanthood an outward leadership attribute? This course will give answers and meanings to these and personal reflective questions to discover the distinguishing characteristics of The Leadership Servanthood attribute. Functional definitions of The Leadership Servanthood attribute and principle will be provided based on the identified characteristics. Readers will benefit from numerous techniques, personal examples, empirical case study, and applications of the concepts.

ALS I Course 10: Trust-Integrity Leadership Attribute—*True leadership trust produces assured trustee's confidence and readiness to follow based on the credibility, competence, and shared relational connections of the trusted.*

A study examined more than 75 key components of employee satisfaction in top leadership and found that trust and confidence was the single most reliable predictor of employee satisfaction in an organization. This course will examine the results of the above study with respect to servant leadership, and how a leader-servant increases the satisfaction of the followers in an organization. When the organization is going through some challenges, how can a leader be credible in helping the followers understand the company's mission and strategy? How can he share information on how the company or institution, or department is doing and how the followers or employees will be affected? Suppose the organization's strategy is not aligned with its inner value or character, how does the leader build trust in followers or earn trust from them? Organizational leadership trust has been defined by as "an employee's willingness to take a risk for a leader with the expectation that, in exchange, the leader will behave in some desired way." The course will examine how the element of reliance and confidence in the actions of the trusted and organization are characterized by a combination of Competence (Can they do the job?), Benevolence (Do they care about me?), and Integrity (Are they honest?).

Referenced Scriptures

A variety of Bible translations from over 11,200 original Hebrew, Aramaic, and Greek words to about 6,000 English words do exist with variations in meanings and emphases. I am not a biblical scholar and do not pretend to be one; Hence, I have avoided researching the roots of these words and personally prefer New King James Version (NKJV). I have intentionally used other translations for three main reasons; first, to allow for increased impact and alignment of words to the most desired meaning and emphasis in the concepts being addressed. Second, I wanted new and personal discovery of meanings from translations with which I have not been familiar. And third, I wanted to allow readers who may desire translations other than the NKJV the benefit of their preferred translations. Hence, in addition to the NKJV, other translations used in the book include New International Version (NIV), New Living Translation (NLT), King James Version (KJV), English Standard Version (ESV), and Good News Translation (GNT). Unless otherwise specified, NKJV should be assumed.

Sylvanus Nwakanma Wosu

CHAPTER 1
UNDERSTANDING LEADERSHIP ATTRIBUTES

Leadership attribute is the combined acts of two or more distinctive functional leadership characteristics exhibited in service and relationship toward others.

The starting point of our discussion is the understanding of the key functional definitions and concepts that describe the theme of this book. In general, 1 will define leadership as an integrative process in which a person applies appropriate attributes to guide and influence the sought-after attitudinal changes in others toward accomplishing a particular goal. Specifically, the Leader as Servant Leadership is a process in which a leader intentionally chooses to put the follower's rights and needs above his positional rights and personal needs, and serves, enables, and empowers them for desired spiritual and professional growth that builds thriving communities.

FUNCTIONAL DEFINITIONS

In the context of these definitions, I will begin the descriptions of the leadership attributes of an authentic leader-servant by offering a functional definition of Leadership Attributes, and showing how that definition differs from those of Leadership Character, Characteristics, and Traits.

Leadership Character is the sum total of personal qualities in leadership, such as honesty, values, vision, trust, and so on that make up the moral capital of the leader; Leadership character should describe who the leader is inside or the leader's basic personality traits.

The Leadership Characteristics describe the distinctive characteristics or features of a leader, such as attitudes, competencies, skills, and specific experiences that go beyond his character (personality). Leadership characteristics determine how (through skills and competencies) the leader leads or take actions in the process of leadership in any particular situation;

The Leadership traits are the distinguishing leadership characteristics of a leader (these are things that define his leadership characteristics), which differentiate from personality traits... Leadership traits are the set of characteristics that define a particular leader's leadership. This means that a leadership characteristic is a trait when it is a unique characteristic of the leader.

Leadership Attributes, unlike leadership character, characteristics, and traits, is *a leadership attribute and the combined act of two or more distinctive functional leadership characteristics exhibited in service and relationship toward others* or traits externally displayed in action toward others. All leadership attributes grow out of the leadership inner value system but can be externally displayed predominantly as an outbound or outward attribute or both:

1. **Outbound Attributes:** These are distinctive outward-bound attributes emanating from the inner strength of the leader to support external conduct in service and relationships toward others. They form the internal core functional qualities that motivate or enhance the outward manifestation of the inside character toward others. The outbound attribute such as listening and vision, for example, are the direct results of the inner values of the leader such as patience, hearing, love, humility, or all the fruits of the spirit.

2. **Outward Attributes:** These are distinctive functional outward outer visible attributes emanating from the richness of the outbound and inner values of the leader. For example, external attributes such as Servanthood, emulation/modeling, empathy, etc. are outflows from the leader who will directly impact the follower. Outward attributes can be enriched by the outbound (inner) attributes. As shown in Figure 1, the outward attributes in general form the outer core of

CHAPTER 1
UNDERSTANDING LEADERSHIP ATTRIBUTES

functional attributes in the leader as servant leadership, but they can share some overlapping functions with the outbound attributes.

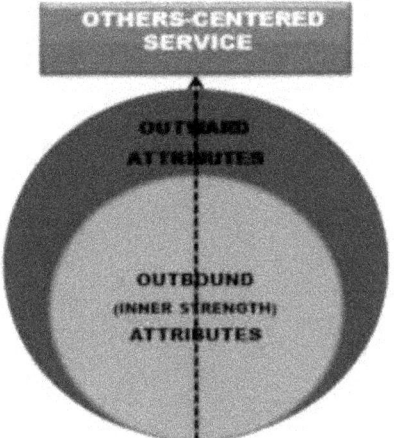

Figure 1.1. Servant leadership functional attributes

In summary, a leadership attribute is more than an ability or a characteristic; it is making those characteristics or abilities functional as part of how the leader acts (his habits) in service to others and applying those characteristics (beyond just having them) in personal and service relations to others. The character or known characteristic defines some aspects of your abilities or who you are inside— e.g. honest, humble, brave, etc. Your attribute, on the other hand, defines your habits; a display of how you use your characteristics, or the actions you exhibit toward others because of who you are inside. For example, empathy as a leadership characteristic becomes a leadership attribute if the followers can distinguish the leader's acts or habits of empathy, such as walking through with his followers in their state of suffering to bring wholeness; otherwise, it is just a characteristic or ability. Leadership attributes toward others are what impact the followers' and the organizational growth more than ability and competence.

In addressing one of the self-righteous hypocritical attributes of servitude leadership, Jesus called leader-servants to be "inside-out" leaders that reflect credibility; indeed, leaders should not appear outwardly righteous when they are full of hypocrisy and lawlessness in their hearts. He was describing "inside–out" as an authentic leadership attribute measured by the display of credibility a leadership attribute!

The measuring stick of a leader-servant is Jesus Christ. We measure ourselves unto the measure of the status of the fullness of Christ (Ephesians 4:13).

The leadership attributes of an authentic leader as a servant are encapsulated in **SERVANT/SERVING LEADERSHIP** are listed in Table 1.1, and defined in Table 1.2: *Servanthood, Emulation, Responsibility, Vision, Navigation, Adaptability, Trust, Listening, Empathy, Affection, Discipleship, Encouragement, Reproduction, Stewardship, Healing-Care, Initiation, Integrity,* and *Persuasion*. Other support attributes include *Influence, Courage, and Generosity*.

The attributes have been separated into Outward and Outbound (Inner Strength) leadership Attributes. As shown in Table 1.1, each of these attributes has three or more leadership characteristics. As such, more than 65 leadership characteristics are covered in these 20 attributes. For example, a leader's Servanthood leadership attribute is characterized by his willing servant's heart of selfless role humility, sacrifice, and submissiveness. The more these are present in a leader, the more effective the servant leadership.

Table 1.1: The functional leader-servant leadership Outbound (Inner Strength) and Outward attributes

	LEADER-SERVANT LEADERSHIP ATTRIBUTES			INNER STRENGTH ATTRIBUTES	OUTWARD ATTRIBUTES
S	Servanthood	L	Listening	Adaptability	Affection
E	Emulation	E	Empathy	Courage	Discipleship
R	Responsibility	A	Affection	Empathy	Emulation
V	Vision	D	Discipleship	Encouragement	Generosity
A	Adaptability	E	Encouragement	Initiation	Healing–Care
N	Navigation	R	Reproduction	Listening	Influence
T	Trust	S	Stewardship	Navigation	Persuasion
I	Influence	H	Healing–Care	Responsibility	Reproduction
G	Generosity	I	Initiation	Stewardship	Servanthood
C	Courage	P	Persuasion	Vision	Trust/Integrity

The list does not assume that a leader has to be excellent in all attributes or even have all of them to be an effective Leader–Servant. However, the more of these attributes the leader displays in his acts of service toward others, the more productive he or she will be, and the further his impact on the followers and organization. The table also shows that two or more attributes can share common characteristics, which can be applied or observed in different contexts. For example, a leader's ability to inspire followers can be seen in his acts of discipleship, empowerment, an.d encouragement attributes in the context in which these attributes apply. Each attribute is exhibited either as a part of the outbound inner strength attribute of a leader or a part of the outward attribute. Table 1.1 is not an exhaustive list of attributes; in fact, there are hundreds of such attributes. This is just the starting point.

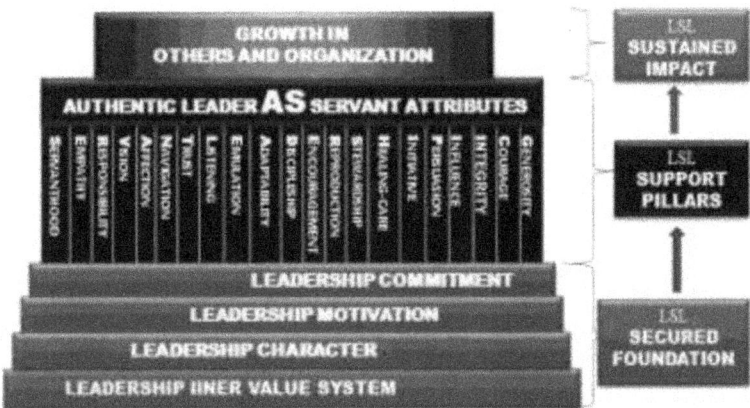

Figure 1.2: Servant leadership outward attributes (dark blue) and relationship to four foundational layers of the LSL Model

Figure 1.2 shows that the leader's attributes are shaped and secured by his four foundational layers (leadership inner value system, leadership character, motivation, and commitment). The attributes of the leader–servants are also conceptualized as the support pillars that will establish and support the personal authenticity of the leader, what the leader, does and the effectiveness of the leadership process. Thus, the attributes represent functional pillars of authentic leadership that can be learned or enriched as described in detail in the subsequent chapters. The combined effect of a secured foundation and stable support pillars will make a sustained impact on the growth of followers and the organization.

COMPARISONS WITH OTHER WORKS

The original works by Greenleaf (1970) in servant leadership [1] have been reviewed by Larry Spears (1996), who identified listening, empathy, healing, awareness, persuasion, conceptualization, foresight, stewardship, commitment to the growth of others, and building community as the ten distinguishing characteristics of servant leadership. [2] Russell (2001) has studied these attributes and have shown them to be essential in servant leadership and concluded that these qualities generally "grow out of the inner values and beliefs of individual leaders." [3] Russell and Stone (2002) extended the Greenleaf 10 attributes to 20 attributes observed in servant-leaders. These 20 attributes were categorized by these authors as either functional attributes (intrinsic characteristics of servant-leaders) or accompanying attributes (complement attributes that enhance the functional attributes).[4] The operational attributes were identified as vision, honesty, integrity, trust, modeling, service, pioneering, appreciation, and empowerment with the accompanying attributes of communication, credibility, competence, stewardship, visibility, influence, persuasion, listening, encouragement, teaching, and delegation. Only three of the attributes identified by Greenleaf were identified, and all three were accompanying attributes rather than functional. Responsibility, adaptability, affection, discipleship, navigation, and reproduction attributes which are considered critical in biblical-based servant leadership in my LSL model are not covered by Russell and Greenleaf. As shown in the description of the attributes in Table 1.2, most of the attributes reported by Russell and Stone (2002)[5] or Greenleaf [1] can be seen either in the twenty attributes or their associated characteristics. Integrity and honesty for example are leadership characteristics of trust and other attributes rather than an independent attributes. I take the position that servant leadership attributes are functional attributes in acts of duty to others and emanate from the inner value system of the leader.

CHAPTER 1
UNDERSTANDING LEADERSHIP ATTRIBUTES

Table 1.2: Description of the functional leader-servant outward leadership attributes and associated principles and characteristics

Leader–Servant Leadership Attributes	Principles of Leadership Attributes	Leadership Characteristics
Affection: *This is the combined love-based works toward providing the essential help or services for the spiritual growth or survival of another person..* (Chapter 2)	*Affection flows from a person to produce positive emotions for the well-being of another person*	Kindness Compassion Practical Love Affective signs Appreciation
Discipleship: *This is the combined acts of personally developing, intentionally equipping, and attentively empowering growth in others to reproduce a heart of service.* (Chapter 3)	*Discipleship transforms and empowers followers for service leadership that grows communities.*	Inspiring Shepherding Equipping Developing Empowering
Emulation: *This is the combined acts of initiating an authentic servant attitude as a model of service worthy of following* (Chapter 4)	*A great leader-servant outwardly and positively inspires a pattern of good works for others to follow.*	Inspiration Motivation Initiation Model Following
Generosity: *This is the combined acts of freely sharing with and giving to others as an act of kindness, without expectation of reward or return to him.* (Chapter 5)	*Generosity is an outward measure of the level of sacrifice, what is shared, or the impact a giving makes, not just the size of the giving.*	Sharing Giving Kindness Affection Love
Healing-Care: *This is the combined acts of providing comfort and empathy to make others whole emotionally and spiritually along with tending to the follower's physical and mental well-being.* (Chapter 6)	*Comforting others in any trouble with the comfort with which we are comforted by God, brings healing - wholeness.*	Self-Healing Empathy Reconciliation Comfort Relational
Influence: *This is the combined acts of positively affecting desired change in conduct,*	*The true measure of leadership success in affecting*	Model Positive attitude Authority

performance, and relational connections toward others-centered course of action or service. (Chapter 7)	*desired change in conduct, performance, and relational connections in others is influence*	Connection Wisdom Intelligence,
Persuasion: *This is the combined acts of communicating perspective to connect, challenge, and convince with a compelling purpose to convert others to a new position.* (Chapter 8)	*The means of transforming others to a new perspective is through empathetic persuasion*	Connecting Challenging Communicating Convincing Converting Encouraging
Reproduction: *This is the combined acts of developing your leadership qualities in others and releasing them as successors to continue a greater mission.* (Chapter 9)	*Great leaders produce successors for legacy and greater courses as an expected product of an effective leadership reproduction.*	Selecting Mentoring Equipping Empowering Releasing
Servanthood: *This is the combined acts of humility, willingness, and intentionality in service to others through selfless sacrifice and submission as a servant.* (Chapter 10)	*A leader-servant is most qualified to lead when most ready to serve as a servant for the growth of others. The role of a leader is to serve as a servant*	Servant's heart Humility Sacrifice Service Willingness Submissiveness
Trust: *This is the combined acts of positive display of character, competence, credibility, and shared relational connections that produce assured trust-confidence of the trustee in the trusted.* (Chapter 11)	*True leadership trust produces assured trustee's confidence and readiness to follow based on the credibility, competence, and shared relational connections of the trusted.*	Character Competence Integrity Credibility Confidence

PRINCIPLE OF LEADERSHIP ATTRIBUTE

In the context of servant leadership, a leadership attribute is a level above the leadership characteristic or trait of a leader. The principle of leadership attribute states that every leadership attribute has a set of distinguishing characteristics that make up the inward or outward display of the attribute. The principle reflects the essential designed purpose or outcome of the attribute or the inevitable consequence of the effective practice of the attribute. Thus, the principle of leadership attribute is a concise statement about the fundamental truth, value, or belief about the attribute in a leadership situation; it is a statement that establishes an idea about the outcome of the attribute for guiding the practical application of the attribute and its characteristics. I will postulate and frame each principle as an additive function of the characteristics of the attribute. A statement of each principle is quoted at the beginning or below the title of each chapter. It is yet to be experimentally proven if the attribute is a linear or some other non-linear function of these characteristics as variables. It is expected, however, that each character will contribute to the effectiveness of the attribute in varying degrees.

AUTHENTIC LEADERSHIP ATTRIBUTES

At a personal level, attributes are the value-based inside-out moral leadership assets that can be related to the authenticity of a leader-servant. The complexity of defining authenticity has been noted in the literature. The subject of authentic leadership is well covered in the works of Terry (1993),[5] George (2003),[6] and Shair and Eilam (2005).[7] All appear to agree that authenticity requires self-awareness and objective self-identity in personal and social interactions with others. In his book, *Advocacy Leadership*, Professor Gary L. Anderson offers individual, organizational, and societal perspectives on authenticity: "Authenticity, at a peculiar level, is living a life, whether in the private or professional term. This is congruent with one's espoused values; at the structural level, authenticity has to do with viewing human beings as ends in themselves, rather than means to other ends; at the public level, it is a state of affairs that is congruous with the shared political and cultural values of society."[8]

The basic tenets of these perspectives are very fitting to authenticity as a qualifying element of leader-servant leadership attributes. The attribute reflects how the followers see the leader based on the leader's distinctive features displayed through his or her actions personally, organizationally, and societally. The leader is seen as a leader-servant or serving leader because the followers see him lead as a servant from an inside-out value of others. This is what makes the leader authentic. Authenticity means that what a leader displays outside, in personal or leadership life of service to others, and society is based on the values the leader espouses inside.

Authenticity in servant leadership can be one or two types or both: *Outbound Authenticity and Outward Authenticity*: The Outbound (outward-bound) Authenticity is the genuineness of personal honesty from your inner strength and abilities; what you say and how you act emanate from who you are or how you feel inside. It reflects the essential truth and honesty about your outward-bound inner strength.

Outward authenticity, on the other hand, describes the truthfulness of your credibility and honesty displayed outward in relation to others; your *outer* visible behavior or how you act outwardly towards others reflects exactly your true intentions.

While *outward* authenticity is the visible *outer* indicator of the truth of who you are inside, *outbound* authenticity is outward-bound attribute from the inside of who you are. Credibility in this context is the influence a leader has to attract believability, trustworthiness, and authenticity; it is the believability, trustworthiness, and authenticity of who you are inside and outside.

A key element of personal authenticity is that it is seen or measured in the context of societal, cultural, and organizational interactions. In that context, achieving individual authenticity becomes a challenge since it is influenced by social factors and dispositions of individuals who usually depend on liberal and organizational realities. However, for leader-servant leadership, the leader can face those changing times by remaining focused on his key Biblical-based principles or *Leadership Inner Value System*. Thus, I am interested in authenticity as an essential element of effective Leader-servant leadership attributes or Leader-servant leadership attributes as drivers of leadership authenticity. With that in mind, the first critical element of authenticity in practicing or developing efficient leader-servant leadership attributes is inside-out self-examination relative to the people served rather than the organization. You may ask yourself: What will be my response when the people I lead act or react in a certain way, will it be negative or positive? What are my strengths and vulnerabilities at those times?

Professor Yacobi in his post, "Elements of Human Authenticity," noted that since "the self -arise attribute emerges from interactions between self, others, and the environment in a complex society and world, there may co-exist multiple complicated identities depending on place and context." [9] He went on to identify the following <u>essential elements of personal authenticity</u>: self-awareness, unbiased self-examination, accurate self-knowledge, reflective judgment, personal responsibility, and integrity, genuineness, and humility, empathy for others, understanding of others, optimal utilization of feedback from others. All of these are covered under the leadership attributes or characteristics shown in Table 1.2.

Bill George, in his book, *Authentic Leadership*, takes the position that to be an authentic leader; a person must have the following essential characteristics: [10]

- Behavior based on value: He must understand his own values and exhibit behavior to others based on those values;
- He must not compromise his values in difficult situations but could use the situation to strengthen personal values in those situations.
- Passion from a clear purpose: Be self-aware of who he is, where he is going, and the right thing to do.
- Compassion from the heart: He must lead from a compassionate heart that allows them to be sensitive to the plight and needs of others,
- Connectedness from a relationship; he must be relationally connected with people he leads,
- Consistency from the self-disciple: He must demonstrate self-discipline to remain calm, collected, and consistent in a stressful situation.

Modeled after the elements above, Table 1.3 lists six essential characteristics of authenticity for servant leadership. These fundamental characteristics cover the five identified above and can also be aligned with the leadership characteristics in Table 1.2. Each attribute in Table 1.2 is expected to pass the personal authenticity test in Tables 1.3, 1.4. In a survey of 132 Christian leaders, seventy-four percent (74%) of them agreed that they always or frequently exhibit servant leadership attributes. [11] Thus, a pass of the outward authenticity test means that a pure leader must demonstrate 70% or more of these essential elements of this legitimacy. (That is, 70% YES in the assessment questions in Tables 1.3, 1.4).

It needs to be noted, however, that a secular leader could be authentic and still lack some of the essential servant leadership attributes or characteristics such as selflessness, servanthood, and love-motivated servant attitudes of a leader-servant. Effective leader-servants are authentic leaders and personal authenticity is an essential element of leader-servant leadership. The key test for leader-servant authenticity is the quality of his inside-out value and personal character. What is most important is a change from the inside-out.

	Table 1.3: The test of essential elements of personal inner strength authenticity in servant leadership		
	Elements of Inner Strength Authenticity	**Inner Strength (Outbound) Authenticity Assessment Questions**	**YES / NO**
1	Personal inside-out value-based behavior	Are your personal inside-out values aligned with acts of service and behavior outside?	1
		Are you honest to yourself in relation to your inner strengths and abilities?	2
2	Inside-out Self-Awareness	Do you have unbiased self-examination, and accurate self-knowledge of who you are inside-out?	3
		Do you know your inner strength and weaknesses in relation to the good you want to show as an outward attribute?	4
3	Inside-out Empathy-Compassion	Do you know and feel from your inside what you want for your followers?	5
		Are you motivated to empathize, based on your inside feelings?	6
4	Inside-out Connection with followers	Do you feel deep, personal, and spiritual connection with your followers?	7
		Does what you say and how you act reflect how you feel when you relate to others?	8
5	Inside-out Emotional Self-regulation	Do you have difficulty controlling your emotion in order to remain calm in a stressful situation?	9
		Are you always able to comfort yourself?	10
6	Inside-out Authenticity Feedback	Do your followers see your inside-out value from your outside behavior?	11
		Will your followers feel that what you say you are is congruent with how you act?	12
	#YESs____ ; # NOs____ : Outbound Authenticity: YES/ 12--------%		

Table 1.4: The test of essential elements of personal outward authenticity in servant leadership

	Elements of Personal Outward Authenticity	Personal Outward Authenticity Assessment Questions	YES or NO
1	Personal value-based outward behavior	Are your personal values and beliefs aligned with your acts of service and behavior toward others?	1
		Do you live out your life according to your beliefs?	2
2	Personal Self-Awareness	Do you have clarity of your personal vision and purpose?	3
		Does what you know about yourself accurately describe what others say?	4
3	Personal Outward Empathy-Compassion	Do you apply how you feel to what your followers need?	5
		Do you lead from a compassionate heart and are you sensitive to the plight and needs of others?	6
4	Personal Connection with followers	Do you feel deep, personal connection with your followers?	7
		Does your outward action toward others reflect exactly your true intentions?	8
5	Outward Emotional Self-regulation	Do you have difficulty controlling your emotions to remain calm in a stressful situation?	9
		Does your evaluation of your value of others agree with how valued they feel?	10
6	Personal Authenticity Feedback	Do your followers see your outward acts as true and honest?	11
		Can your followers see other-centeredness in 70% or more of your attributes?	12

#YESs_____; # NOs_____; Outward Authenticity: YES/ 12———%

ALS TRUST-INTEGRITY LEADERSHIP
ATTRIBUTES, PRINCIPLES, & PRACTICES

SUMMARY 1
UNDERSTANDING LEADERSHIP PROCESS

The following set of questions is designed to serve as a guide to discover, explore, and practice the essential ALS leadership attributes, principles, and practices in leadership process. The questions are comprehensive review based on the content of this chapter only.

To maximize the learning outcomes, the learner must read through this chapter and sections. Some referenced scriptures in the book are repeated in the summaries for added review if needed, even though they were discussed in the section in which they apply.

All answers to the questions are contained in the associated chapter or sections; consultation of new sources is not needed. Thus, it is expected that you answer the questions after you have read the book.

Discovering the Leadership Attributes

Table 1.5. Leader As Servant-Leadership Audit						
A servant-leader in his leadership position purposefully choses to serve and inspire acts of service in others by his example. Select and circle best answer to questions						
1=Never: 2=Almost never ; 3=Sometimes; 4=Frequently; 5 =Always						
	Servant Leadership assessment questions	Circle no				
1	I am willing and other-centered, and readily chose to serve others as a servant for their personal growth	1	2	3	4	5
2	I model others-centered attitude in my service and relationships and inspire same for others to follow	1	2	3	4	5
3	I have a sense of obligation, willingness, and accountability for the service towards others	1	2	3	4	5
4	I have the foresightedness to specify in the present view what others' growth should be in a given future	1	2	3	4	5
5	I work toward providing the essential help or services for the spiritual growth or survival of the others;	1	2	3	4	5
6	I provide the needed purposeful course of action for how to chart the course to for my followers.	1	2	3	4	5
7	I display external credibility and a strong sense of character based on values, beliefs, and competence;	1	2	3	4	5
8	In communication, I attentively perceive and hear what is communicated, reflectively listen to understand and to be understood	1	2	3	4	5

CHAPTER 1
UNDERSTANDING LEADERSHIP ATTRIBUTES

#	Statement	1	2	3	4	5
9	I walk through with others in their state (suffering, emotions, etc.) in a way that provides the needed care and well-being	1	2	3	4	5
10	I have a measure of self-secured flexibility to adapt appropriate attitude to serve all people in different situations	1	2	3	4	5
11	I personally develop, intentionally equip, and attentively nurture spiritually growth in others	1	2	3	4	5
12	My act of bravery instills in others the courage and confidence to follow or persevere in a course of action	1	2		4	5
13	I develop my leadership qualities in others as successors to continue in a purposeful mission	1	2	3	4	5
14	I manage, maintain,, and account for all resources entrusted to me and being responsible for the difference my acts make	1	2	3	4	5
15	As a care-giver, I act to comfort and make others whole emotionally	1	2	3	4	5
16	When I see a need, I originate a vision and action, and stay committed to meet that need and desired change	1	2	3	4	5
17	I display a holistic view of an issue to inform, transform or convert others to my view through empathetic persuasion	1	2	3	4	5
18	I freely share what I have sacrificially as an act of kindness to others, without expectation of reward in return	1	2	3	4	5
19	My act of influence is to affect the actions, behavior, opinions, etc., of others based on trust, credibility and relationship	1	2	3	4	5
20	In the face challenges and danger, I act with bravery to overcome fear and take a stand with strength and conviction	1	2	3	4	5
Score Range	Add up the numbers in each column (Total Score____ Check and Understand the key areas to work on					
81-100	Strong Leader-Servant; keep it up, go and train others.					
66-80	Above average Leader-Servant; work 25% of key areas					
50-65	Average but developing; need to work on 50% of key areas					
34-49	Below average leader; work on 75% of key areas					
<34	Not a Leader-Servant; need training in all areas					

CHAPTER 2
LEADERSHIP TRUST-INTEGRITY ATTRIBUTE

True leadership trust produces assured trustee's confidence and readiness to follow based on the credibility, competence, and shared relational connections of the trusted.

Lamb and McKee (2004) in their book, *Applied Public Relations*, cited a 2001 study conducted by the Hay Group, a global human-resource management consultancy group, worldwide. The study examined more than 75 key components of employee satisfaction in top leadership and found that trust and confidence was the single most reliable predictor of employee satisfaction in an organization. [55] The study also showed that effective communication by leadership in three critical areas that are key to winning organizational trust and confidence:

(1) Helping employees understand the company's overall business strategy;
(2) Helping employees understand how they contribute to achieving key business objectives; and
(3) Sharing information with employees on how the company is doing and how an employee's division is doing relative to strategic business objectives.

Examining the results of the above study with respect to servant leadership, how can a leader-servant increase the satisfaction of the followers in an organization? When the organization is going through some challenges, how can a leader be credible in helping the followers understand the company's mission and strategy? How can he share information on how the company or institution or department is doing and how the followers or employees will be affected? Suppose the organization's strategy is not aligned with its inner value or character, how does the leader build trust in followers or earn trust from them?

CHARACTERISTICS OF TRUST ATTRIBUTE

Organizational leadership trust has been defined by Kenexa High-Performance Institute as "an employee's *willingness* to take a risk for a leader with the expectation that, in exchange, the leader will *behave* in some desired way."[56] The expectation in the above definition supposes that trust requires the element of *reliance* and *confidence* in the actions of the trusted without monitoring by the trustee. The willingness is motivated by those expectations and not coerced by the employee. According to Kenexa High-Performance Institute and other organizational experts, organization trust and distrust are characterized by a combination of Competence (Can they do the job?), *Benevolence* (Do they care about me?), and *Integrity* (Are they honest?) which together account for about 80 percent of what makes employees' trust their leaders. A 2011 WorkTrends survey by the same group and based on a sub-sample of 10,000 employees from the U.S, showed that of these three qualities, "integrity is the most important at 41 percent, followed by benevolence at 34 percent, then competence at 25 percent." [56] This result reveals that while leaders' competence or knowing how to do their jobs well is important, the employees also want the leaders to display honesty, value, and care toward them. I take the position that benevolence as an act of value and care is borne out of the empathetic and *relational connection* between leaders and their followers or employees. According to the same WorkTrends survey report, Forty-eight (48) percent of all US employees trusted their leaders, with 28 percent and 24 percent actively distrusted their leaders and undecided, respectively. Such results are not surprising given the current trend of power-centered leadership apathy to the needs of employees. One solution is a shift to a leader-servant leadership model. A 2013 survey of 132 non-denominational Christian practicing leaders ranked trust/integrity as the 3rd (out of 17) most important leadership attribute (see Table 2.1) with 62 percent agreeing that they are *always* others-centered in their trust servant leadership. [54] Overall, more than 81% of these leaders perceive themselves to be leader-servants who put others' needs above theirs in service leadership.

Good relational connections or relationships that empower growth in people and organizations are based on *true trust* on several different levels. Robbins (2005) in his book, *Organizational Behavior,* [57] identified three types of trust in an organizational relationship: *deterrence*-based, a trust based on fear of reprisal if the trust is violated; *knowledge*-based, which exists when the leader is understood based on adequate information about the leader; and *identification*-based, trust when there is an emotional connection between the parties. Trust in Servant leadership can be identification-based or knowledge-based. Jesus developed trust in his followers through close and regular interactions with them to allow them to know him more. Identification-based trust is developed through empathy and an emotional connection between the parties. According to Robbins, this type of trust is enhanced by mutual understanding between the parties.

Stephen Covey stated "The foundation of trust is your own *credibility*, and it can be a real differentiator for any leader... Trust is *"confidence* born of two dimensions: *character* and *competence*." [58] The credibility of the leader-servant is the result of the inner *character* of the leader based on his *value* system.

Credibility in all of its forms is a function of one's *integrity,* where integrity in this context refers to the measure of the wholeness of the honesty, truthfulness, and character of a leader seen by others with respect to the values the leader espouses. But the quality of integrity, character, and competence a leader displays increases the quality of the confidence people have in the leader. Thus, the trusted credibility or believability of the leader is to the level of his integrity. Patrick Lencioni in his book, *Five Dysfunctions of a Team,* examined how trust is the basic foundation upon which teams and organizations thrive.[59] James Choung in citing this work noted: "integrity is a deal-breaker: the lack of integrity will be a surefire way to create distrust, animosity, and apathy. Without trust, a leader has no authority to influence." [60] These studies set the context for framing the principle of leadership trust attribute.

PRINCIPLE OF LEADERSHIP TRUST ATTRIBUTE

True trust produces *confidence* and readiness to follow. Such confidence does not exist in the presence of a negative track record or the leader's inability to correct that track record instead of justifying the record. Just as God entrusts in us a measure of authority to empower others, a leader must also trust the people he serves without prejudging their responses. The primary distinguishing leadership characteristics of servant leadership trust attribute are credibility, *character, integrity, relational connection,* and *competence*. These can be defined as follows:

> *Servant leadership trust attribute is the combined acts of positive display of character, competence, credibility, and shared relational connections that produce assured trust-confidence of the trustee in the trusted.*

The *confidence* that followers have in a leader is a direct result or measure of their trust in a leader. The above definition means that the trust attribute is a mutually interdependent leader-follower outward interaction. That is, trust can be formed when a leader leads by first extending trust to followers. Followers readily extend trust to a leader when a leader displays such leadership characteristics as commitment, competence, credibility, vision, and benevolence based on the leader's relational connection. Trusting followers eagerly follow a trusting leader. Thus, building trust requires diligence and attention to cultivating behaviors that lead to trust over time. A leader's trust is the capital that builds followers' confidence in him and their readiness to follow him.

> *Servant leadership trust principle: True leadership trust produces an assured trustee's confidence and readiness to follow based on the credibility, competence, and shared relational connections of the trusted.*

This principle means that trust is developed, earned, or given when the quality of the trustee's confidence in the leader's competence, credibility, and relational connection in service to others inspires assuredness in the trustee's willingness to follow. Stated differently, trust-confidence is the instinctive assuredness of the character, competence, relational connection, and credibility of the trusted based on a sound value system. The servant leadership trust principle is expressed as:

CHARACTER + COMPETENCE+ INTEGRITY + CREDIBILITY = TRUST

The relationship between the four characteristic dimensions leading to trust-confidence is modeled as an additive four-stage process in Figure 8:
- **Develop Character**
- **Build Competence**
- **Ensure Integrity**
- **Display Credibility**

Trust starts from developing or training your character from the inward moral capital of the leader. The character developed from a sound value-based foundation builds the value-based competence of the leader measured by his culture of excellence, knowledge, intelligence, philosophy, etc. The external outcome of leadership trust attribute is credibility measured by the display of integrity, motive, good report, etc.

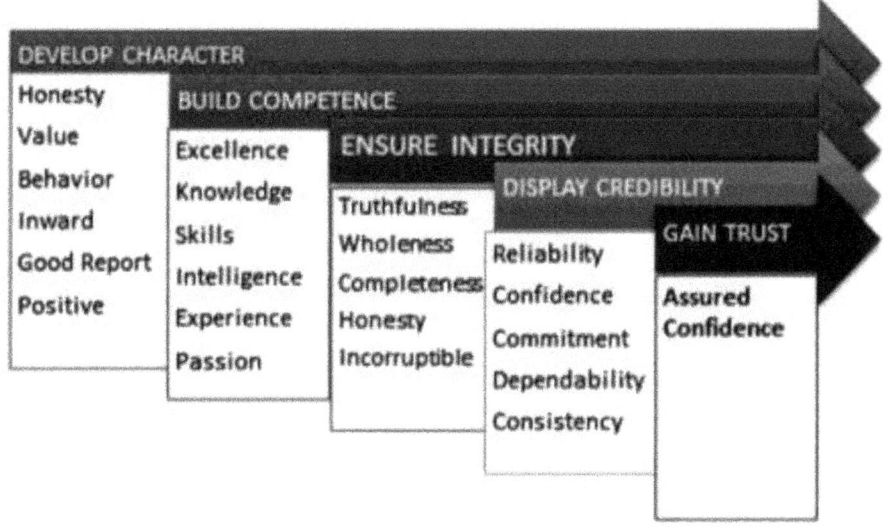

Figure 11: Additive process model of servant leadership trust-attribute

SUMMARY 2
LEADERSHIP TRUST-INTEGRITY ATTRIBUTE

Before starting this exercise, please read and follow the instruction in the preface of this workbook. Answers to these questions are contained in this chapter. Completion of these exercises after reading the chapter should take 60-90 minutes.

Discovering Trust-integrity leadership attribute

1. Define trust with respect to organizational leadership. What are the key elements in the definition of trust
2. What is the role of Trust in relational connections or relationships that empower growth
3. According to Robbins [57] what are three types of trust in an organizational relationship:
4. How is Trust in Servant leadership identified as identification-based or knowledge-based..
5. What is the foundation of trust according to Stephen Covey [58] and on what is the foundation based
6. Credibility in all of its forms is a function of one's *integrity*. *In this context, what is* integrity?

Understanding the principle of Trust-integrity leadership attribute

1. Define Trust leadership attribute.
2. Sate the principle of Trust leadership Attribute
3. What are the primary distinguishing leadership characteristics of servant trust leadership attribute
4. How leadership trust is developed, earned, or given State the additive law or process of trust leadership attribute
5. How are the characteristic of trust related to he level of the confidence people have in the leader. What is the role of Trust in leadership influence.

CHAPTER 3
DEVELOPING TRUST-CHARACTER

Trust- character is any quality that builds the leader's ability to trust the followers or earn the trust of the followers. Such character qualities include integrity, truthfulness, motivation, and consistency. The level of trust a leader earns from others is built on his integrity. In this context, integrity can be seen as the quality of his inner character consistently applied in how he behaves externally in his act of serving others and in the organization. Trust character is learned or can be trained. Here are a few strategies to consider:

Develop a sound values system

A leader's character is based on his values, and there are several values important in leadership. However, trust values are those that form the foundational characteristics that build trust in leadership. The leader's trust values are what hold his character and competence in check. These values include diligence, faith, virtue, knowledge, self-control, perseverance, kindness, and love. A leader is secure in his abilities based on these values and sound moral principles. Such a strong sense of security earns him the trust of others. A leader's value affects his self-efficacy; that is, his belief in his power and competence through faith to produce desired outcomes. The quality of these outcomes increases people's confidence in him. Self-efficacy bore out from a strong value system and experiences the effects, not only the power a person has to face challenges competently, but also the choices a person is most likely to make in a given situation. Leaders with high self-efficacy are more likely to have a lofty sense of security, which leads followers to trust them more.

Develop positive character traits

Develop positive character traits to build people's trust. Trust is fundamental in military service and is embedded in the military's core leadership principles. The leader's ability to build trust is measured by a good sense of character, which is composed of beliefs, values, skills, and traits. [61] He must clearly communicate the overall organization's goals, objectives, and strategies: Help others understand the overall business strategy. An effective way to fully communicate this is through a strategic planning retreat that engages all units in your *direct circle of influence*. The key actions must include:

- *Help others understand* how they can engage and contribute to achieving key business objectives. After the team, members understand the comprehensive goal and the method of assessing how they can contribute to the goals, individual units and members of the team should be guided through a strategic planning retreat to develop and align their peculiar goals to overall missions and goals.
- *Sharing information* is an effective way to provide open channels of communication. This is access to information that organizational members need to meet their tasks and to be successful. Build trust by openly and honestly sharing information with employees to understand their concerns and interests regarding critical changes that will impact their lives. This shows the organization cares.
- *Maintaining confidentiality* is an important element of effective communication between leaders and their followers. Certain personal information must be kept confidential. Sharing such information with others is often leaked as gossip in the hands of people that see an opportunity to defame a fellow worker. These actions by a leader is a direct and effective way to lose the trust of the victim and others in the organization. Speak the truth to your followers in love; they desire absolute honesty and openness from their leaders no matter how painful the information might be.

Commit to integrity and sound judgments

Leaders must commit to honesty, integrity, and sound judgments. Honesty, integrity, and sound judgment function together to externally display the trust and credibility of a leader. It matters very little how strong a leader is in the other four competency skills discussed above if honesty, integrity, and sound judgment are missing from the character of a leader. In fact, they define what makes us the "salt" described by Jesus. "If the salt has lost its flavor, how shall it be seasoned? It is neither fit for the land nor for the dunghill, but men throw it out" (Luke 14: 35, NKJV) Honesty and integrity are the bonding glue that cements all the leadership attributes for the external reputation of the leader. A compromise on your honesty and integrity could be a downward slope to the ladder of your leadership trust.

Create value for diversity and inclusiveness

People work best when they feel valued. People feel most valued when they are included. People who feel included regardless of their differences develop a sense of empowerment. When people feel valued, included, and empowered, they can trust and engage with others to build relationships in which they work interdependently and synergistically. Valuing the diversity of both people and perspectives increases trust and productivity. Here are some ways to achieve this goal:

- *Explore, identify, and value* the group differences. Listen actively, openly, and respectfully to others. Show that you understand the key challenges your followers are facing.
- *Manage cultural differences* as a joint trust-building opportunity. Be open to other people's ideas and perspectives by fostering a respectful environment in which ideas flourish, and the structure has the flexibility to accommodate new ideas and provide regular opportunities for collective action.
- *Increase cultural competence and sensitivity.* Recognize multiple perspectives on an event or behavior, identify one's values and those of others, and develop a positive attitude toward understanding and appreciating the cultural difference that promotes appropriate behaviors.
- *Foster links between the mission and the practices* of the group community. This requires the ability to speak the language of others in the community; that is, get to know the people, understand their culture, and how they discuss ideas differently, Capitalize on the diverse strengths that distinctive members of the community bring to the effort, and understanding how everyone can work together in the various spheres of responsibility to translate ideas into action.
- *Develop a community-wide culture* that supports free-flowing ideas. This encourages collective efforts within the community and recognizes the need for ongoing reflection and renewal. Make intentional efforts for people to collaborate around a common goal and show that you value others' contributions through an effective reward system.

SUMMARY 3
DEVELOPING THE ACT OF TRUST-CHARACTER

Before starting this exercise, please read and follow the instruction in the preface of this workbook. Answers to these questions are contained in this chapter. Completion of these exercises after reading the chapter should take 60-90 minutes.

Discovering the act of Trust-Character attribute

1. Define trust-character. Give example character qualities how is the level of trust a leader earns from others built on his integrity. In this context, how is integrity the quality of inner character
2. How can trust character be learned or can be trained.
3. A leader's character is based on his values; trust values are those that form the foundational characteristics that build trust in leadership. List some of such values and how does a leader develop a sound value system.

Practicing the Acts of Trust Character

1. How does a leader build sense of security and increase people's confidence in him..
2. How do you develop positive character traits to build people's trust.
3. The leader's ability to build trust is measured by a good sense of character, which is composed of beliefs, values, skills, and traits. [61]
4. What are some effective ways to communicate the overall organization's
5. *How is maintaining confidentiality* an important element of effective communication between leaders and their followers.
6. Leaders must commit to honesty, integrity, and sound judgments. How do these three function together to externally display the trust and credibility of a leader.
7. What are some ways that valuing the diversity of both people and perspectives increases trust and productivity.

CHAPTER 4
BUILDING TRUST-COMPETENCE

In addition to character, competence is a fundamental dimension of trust. Competence can be defined as "the leader's ability to *say* it, *plan* it, and *do* it in a way that others know you, know your business, and know that they want to follow." [26] Trust competencies is the leader's ability to base his action on moral principles and good judgment and complete a task in a way that makes people trust him. Trust competences are those qualities such as behaviors, skills, knowledge, capabilities, and emotional intelligence that influence a person's confidence, build the person's trust to complete a duty properly, and help earn him trust of others. Trust competence can be measured by the leader's performance results and track record relative to the leader's set of competencies. Trust and confidence in a leader or follower are built over time. The life of Moses and Joshua serve as typical examples. Moses did not even believe in himself and found it hard to agree with God that he could be competent enough for God's agenda for the deliverance of Israel from Egypt. However, God provided him with all that he needed to be a strong leader. Moses mentored and prepared Joshua for leadership but God built the competency skills of Joshua, beginning with trusting him enough to head the military campaigns from the wilderness into Canaan to leading the nation of Israel as a transformed leader (Joshua 11:16-23; Numbers 13:16).

Jesus also worked on selecting the disciples. He could trust. . Here are five competency skills or actions to build trust from Jesus' teaching (Luke 14:27-35):

Build commitment and trust attitude

Leaders and followers must commit to what matters. To build trust for people to follow, a leader must let the followers understand what matters most to him and demonstrate his commitment to that purpose. Furthermore, a follower must show his willingness personally to sacrifice and commit to the leader and his mission. Jesus demonstrated both: His work of salvation with the expressed love for humanity was important enough to Jesus and the Father who sent Him that He gave His life for it. Here in this teaching He says, "And whoever does not bear his cross and come after Me cannot be My disciple" (Luke 14:27, NKJV). The willingness to leave all to follow Jesus is not only a measure of our commitment but also of a trusting attitude that says, "I will sacrifice all to follow you because you matter enough for me to trust all to you." That is the attitude the Lord was expecting from them, and all of us that aspire to be leader-servants.

Create a good plan to finish strong

The ability to plan well to finish strong as a competence skill means spending time, in the beginning, to prepare, measure and understand the resources (talents, cost, abilities, time) at hand, how and where, to effectively use them. "For which of you, intending to build a tower, does not sit down first and count the cost, whether he has enough to finish it—lest, after he has laid the foundation, and is not able to finish, all who see it begin to mock him" (Luke 14:28-29, NKJV). Hardly will followers want to trust and have confidence in a leader who never finishes what he starts. Such a leader is a mockery of effective leadership vision and accountability. Your competency that builds trust or shows how strong you will finish is judged by your few completed initiatives rather than by the several initiatives you started but never finished.

Be prudent in your decision

Being thoughtful, intelligent, and prudent in your decision is an important competency skill to know what to, how to, when to, be capable of, and where to start to do a project; it is the hallmark of the farsightedness of a bright visionary leader. Jesus asked; "What king, going to make war against another king, does not sit down first and consider whether he is able with ten thousand to meet him who comes against him with twenty thousand? or else, while the other is still a great way off, he sends a delegation and asks conditions of peace" (Luke 14:31-32, NKJV) The important emphasis, here is to be prudent and thoughtful about your abilities. It is a display of prudence not to initiate an action because you lack the abilities or what is needed, but it is unwise to quickly initiate the action and not finish it. Retreating from a purpose due to thoughtless hasty initiation is a display of incompetency and an easy way to lose the trust of your followers. Jesus wanted to trust only those who would commit to joining with Him fully in the ministry as disciples; nevertheless, they must first measure, understand, and be able to bear the cost to follow him emotionally and physically. Jesus sums it up this way: "Whoever of you does not forsake all that he has cannot be My disciple." (Luke 14:33, NKJV). Why? He desires to be first above all else; He deserved to be the primary; and our priorities must be about His mission agenda, not ours.

Pursue excellence as the choice.

Great leaders pursue excellence and do not settle for average. Make excellence a lifestyle by continually improving, paying attention to details, and showing genuine and consistent respect for others. In my experience over the years, I have always seen that followers and most leaders are easily drawn toward those individuals who pursue excellence in whatever they do. Jesus said, "Salt is good; but if the salt has lost its flavor, how shall it be seasoned? (Luke 14:34, NKJV). This means that a tasteless salt is worthless in the purpose for which it is intended to serve. Why would a follower trust a leader that is always at the marginal end of a continuum for excellence? To be great in what God has purposed for you, you must trust and follow those that pursue excellence. In our academic business, the quality of your graduate research work is usually aligned with the reputation of the institution or the leader who supervised the project.

SUMMARY 4
DEVELOPING THE ACTS OF TRUST-COMPETENCE

Before starting this exercise, please read and follow the instruction in the preface of this workbook. Answers to these questions are contained in this chapter. Completion of these exercises after reading the chapter should take 60-90 minutes.

Discovering the Acts of Trust-Competence

1. Define competence in the context of trust. How is competence a fundamental dimension of trust. Competence can be defined

as "the leader's ability to say it, plan it, and do it in a way that others know you, know your business, and know that they want to follow." 26
2. Define Trust competence and give examples
3. How do you measure Trust competence
4. Trust and confidence in a leader or follower is built over time. How the life Moses and Joshua serve as typical examples. (Joshua 11:16-23; Numbers 13:16) or the life of Jesus and His disciples (Luke 14:27-35):

Practicing the Acts of Trust-Competence

1. What must Leaders and followers do to commit to what matters. How did Jesus demonstrate commitment to His mission? (Luke 14:27, NKJV).
2. How do you create a good plan to finish strong as competence skills? How did Jesus demonstrate this strategy? (Luke 14:28-29, NKJV).
3. How do you judge your competency that builds trust or shows how strong you will finish
4. Being thoughtful, intelligent, and prudent in your decision is an important competency skill to know what to, how to, when to, be capable of, and where to start to do a project; what did Jesus illustrate this principle in (Luke 14:31-32, NKJV).
5. Pursue excellence as the choice for building trust-competence. How do great leaders pursue excellence and do not settle for average and make excellence a lifestyle

CHAPTER 5
DEVELOPING THE ACTS OF TRUST-INTEGRITY

Trust-Integrity is the element of integrity that ensures the believability and trustworthiness of the leader. Ethically, integrity is generally described as the outward acts of honesty and truthfulness of a person or "adherence to moral and ethical principles; soundness of virtuous character; honesty" according to dictionary.reference.com. The word "integrity" comes from the Latin root word "integer," which means "whole" "complete" or "entire." In this context, integrity can refer to the total honesty and truthfulness of one's actions.

Understand wholeness and the life of Integrity

In the Bible, from the Hebrew word, integrity was defined as "the condition of being without blemish, completeness, perfection, sincerity, soundness, uprightness, wholeness" Old Testament. It is used as the "honesty and adherence to a pattern of good works" in the New Testament. [62] Thus, a person has integrity when the person's actions. are judged by others to be congruent with values and beliefs the person espouses or is expected to hold. A person of integrity is a whole person whose outward character matches the inside, and the actions represent the complete or entire words with nothing hidden. By these definitions above, can one find a leader that can be considered to have integrity –be perfect without blemish, whole, and consistently incorruptible? You can only find such a person in Jesus Christ. Even as a man, He is an authentic model of integrity:

He was blemished and incorruptible. As we have already discussed, one of the elements of Jesus's character that Satan attacked at the beginning of His ministry was His integrity using three deceitful means. Satan tempted Him in His most vulnerable human state—hungry and tired after 40 days and 40 nights in the desert. However, He stood against Satan and never sinned. Satan's tactic was to blemish his record using the usual human desires—sustenance, fame, and power. In each case, He was without sin, without blemish, perfectly and completely truthful in all His ways. Jesus lived a perfect sinless life that until today is unmatched as to what a complete life of character and integrity, and positive influence because of those qualities should be. A blemish in life is the result of sin and no matter how great a leader could be in our world; that leader cannot be without sin. "For all men have sinned, and come short of the Glory of God" (Rom. 3:23). Only Jesus was without sin. Yes, He was 100% God, but He was also 100% human who lived without sin (Hebrew 4:15). He left us a pattern of good works to which we must adhere and follow. No wonder Apostle Paul wrote that we were created for excellent works to which we must labor.

He was the truth and pattern of truth for a life of integrity. If an element of integrity is truth, then Jesus is a good model because He represents the only authentic truth according to the Bible. He is the whole truth and the light of life (John 14:6). He represents truth in all of its forms. The only way a man can come close to having integrity is through the power of the Holy Spirit through Jesus. To follow a pattern of truth, we must follow Jesus' Model. Jesus showed us a model of humility and Servanthood. Jesus came at a time when greatness was by lording power over others and taught that greatness comes through humility and serving others. But not only teaching it He lived His life in service of others.

Pursue a model life of integrity

Apostle Paul after his encounter with Jesus pursued a life of integrity following the life of Jesus. Paul not only committed himself to the gospel message, he actually practiced it, and it became an absolute part of his life. Paul's life of integrity was to be found complete, and he chose to live, in Christ and to die for that conviction that to him was a valuable gain, according to Paul. That is pure integrity! Writing to the Corinthians, Paul said; "For we aim at what is honorable not only in the Lord's sight but also in the sight of man" (2 Corinthians 8:21, ESV). He was very intentional; his measure of integrity was the Lord's standard and not by man. To the Ephesian Church, he said; "Not by the way of eye-service, as people-pleasers, but as servants of Christ, doing the will of God from the heart" (Ephesians 6.6, ESV). This was Paul exhorting believers to think of ways to remain unpolluted, positive, and genuine to themselves. Notes these words: "Finally, brothers, whatever is true, whatever is honorable, whatever is just, whatever is pure, whatever is lovely, whatever is commendable, if there is any excellence, if there is anything worthy of praise, think about these things" (Philippians 4:8, ESV).

One important lesson we learned from Apostle Paul was that a critical characteristic of integrity is consistency. A life of integrity must be incongruent with values and beliefs the person espouses or is expected to hold inside and outward. A life of integrity is consistent with the person's character and convictions. Apostle Paul's passion was to complete the race that he believed Christ set before him no matter the difficulties and affirmatives life threw at him. Paul remained true to his values, beliefs, and convictions to complete the race and demonstrated a pattern for us as leaders; we must complete the purpose and rejoice in them even in the state of suffering that we might face.

The apostle Peter also recognized that integrity can only come through consistently living out Jesus' examples, Peter said, "Let him who means to love life and see good days refrain his tongue from evil and his lips from speaking guile. And let him turn away from evil and do good; Let him seek peace and pursue it. For the eyes of the Lord are upon the righteous, And His ears attend to their prayer, But the face of the Lord is against those who do evil" (1 Peter 3:10-12, NKJV).

Live with wholeness and integrity

Authentic leaders live with wholeness and integrity for trust and authority. The effectiveness of any leader-servant from Biblical times until today is directly linked to a life of integrity. Most leaders failed the test of integrity; from the time of Adam through Abraham to David and Moses, here are a few of these leaders who failed in some instances in their test of integrity. Adam, not living up to the responsibility entrusted to him by God, allowed his wife to usurp authority and ignored the instructions God had given to him and this brought his failure, his fall, and the fall of humanity (Genesis 4); Abraham telling one lie or half-truth after the other, such as when he told half-truth about Sarai his wife (Genesis 12) and not patient with the plan of God for an heir and had Ismael with Sarai's maid, which started the first dysfunctional family due to the rivalry between Sarai and Hagar her maid (Genesis 16); David, when Kings go to war stayed to commit adultery with beautiful Bathsheba and sinned against God (2 Samuel 11,12, 13); Moses lost his consistent work with God when he disobeyed God and abused the power God gave to him; instead of speaking to the rock for water as God had instructed, he stroke the rock (Numbers 20:7-11). All these leaders and many more failed in their tests of integrity and never finished strong. The failures or successes of these Biblical leaders and more are directly tied to how they lived. Whenever each of these leaders lived in integrity and wholeness before God and the people, they served, they were blessed or they all suffered when they did not.

The above short historical review of some Biblical leaders sets up a very clear principle of integrity leadership: Leaders with integrity live with wholeness and assuredness to finish strong. This explains why Apostle Paul focused on the training of the character of leaders like Timothy and Titus because a life of integrity makes a leader complete to the extent of the strength of character or moral code of conduct of the leader. A leader's virtuous capital makes up his integrity patterns or code of conduct. Paul recognized the importance of moral capital and the priorities a leader should have. Leaders are required to be people of the highest caliber above reproach (1 Timothy 3:1–3; Titus 2:1–4; II Peter 3:14–15).

Live out integrity by a code of conduct

Authentic leaders live out a life of integrity by a code of conduct. Integrity is a part of your wholeness means that you must consistently and diligently demonstrate to your followers internally and externally that you are complete, blemish, and incorruptible by the following code of conduct:

(1) **Above Reproach.** This is the ability to live above blame from followers and outsiders. You must demonstrate integrity and break free from the habits that defile your character through the "works of the flesh" (Galatians 5:19-21)

(2) **Temperate**. Have the ability to be modest and sober-minded in all things; demonstrate a level of comfort in yourself.

(3) **Self-controlled.** This is the ability to take charge, discipline your life, and self-regulate your emotions, actions, and

reactions that could negatively affect your behavior internally and externally.

(4) **Respectable.** Demonstrate the ability to command respect and esteem from followers and outsiders based on your observable external behavior and the life you live.

(5) **Faithful.** This means being unchanging to his wife as well as leading his family well. Paul sets this quality as a test for leadership. If you cannot oversee your immediate family, Paul questions how you can oversee followers who are not immediate families.

(6) **Good testimony.** Before outsiders, have the ability to demonstrate an excellent reputation to outsiders and a valid report of a godly lifestyle as measured by being above reproach in the above other qualities.

(7) **Be of high moral standard in your choices.** You must avoid drunkenness and violence (Titus 1:7). This is set as a serious flaw in any leader's character that is enough for the leader to be rejected because of the far-reaching, controlling effect of strong drinks.

(8) **Peace-loving and having an interpersonal attitude**. You must avoid having a quarrelsome attitude. The inability to get along with people will strongly impact a leader's ability to lead and can be the result of a much more serious character flaw such as pride, power control, or lack of love, all of which go against the qualities expected of a Servant–Leader.

(9) **A good steward and generous service attitude toward money.** Having too much attachment to money and wealth could lead to irresponsibility, and lack of generosity for service, and can compromise a leader's stewardship of God's resources.

Other Biblical leaders also modeled integrity and obedient submission to God. Table 5.1 shows a short list of characteristics of a person that can be considered to have integrity with wholeness and completeness:

Table 5.1: Characteristics of Integrity in a leader		
	Characteristics of a Leader with Integrity. The Leader…..	Bible References
1	Walks securely,	Proverbs 10:9
2	Is Upright and not crooked	Proverbs 11:3
3	Works heartily in all things	Colossians 3:23
4	Is faithful in a everything, big or little	Luke 16:10
5	Is forward and straight and turns away from evil.	Proverbs 4:25-27
6	Aims at what is honorable in sight of God and man.	2 Corinthians 8:21
7	Has clear conscience and acts honorably in all things.	Hebrews 13:18
8	Delights in God's and righteousness.	Psalm 41:11-12
9	Has a clear heart, blameless, Speaks truth and not utter deceit	Job 27:4-6
10	Holds fast to righteousness before God and man	
11	Keeps good and honorable conduct with others	1 Peter 2:12
12	Is a good and humble steward above reproach	Titus 1:7
13	Waits on God with uprightness	Psalm 25:21
14	Will not act to be defiled even when others do	Daniel 1:8-20
15	Trusts in the Lord without wavering.	Psalm 26:1
16	Is hospitable, a lover of good, self-controlled, upright,	Titus 1:8 s
17	Is Pure heart and a good conscience and a sincere faith.	1 Timothy 1:5
18	Is Trustworthy, consistent, incorruptible, not slanderous and does no evil; Walks blamelessly, and speaks truth from heart;	Psalm 15:1-5
19	Has a clear conscience toward God and man.	Acts 24:16
20	Does the will of God from the heart,	Ephesians 6:6
21	Works on the cleanness of his hands	Psalm 18:20
23	Does justice and love kindness, and walk humbly	Micah 6:8

24	Walks in God's faithfulness.	Psalm 26:1-3
25	Has clean hands and a pure heart and no falsehood	Psalm 24:3-5
26	Refuses to practice cunning or to tamper with God's word	2 Corinthians 4:2
27	Is not an eye-server but with sincerity of heart, fearing the Lord.	Colossians 3:22
28	Does not walk with falsehood and deceit;	Job 31:1-40
29	Models of good works in all respect—teaching, integrity, dignity	Titus 2:7
30	Lives a whole life always in all good conscience	
31	Is clothed in righteousness and justice, and walks uprightly	Job 29:14
32	Despises evil and takes no bribe	Isaiah 33:15
33	Will not transgress the law.	Psalm 17:3
34	Holds fast to integrity no matter the situation	Job 13:15
35	Truly execute justice one with another,	Jeremiah 7:5
36	Steadfast and faithful in his heart.	Proverbs 3:3
37	Not greedy and collect no more than is authorized	Luke 3:13
38	Does according to all that God has commanded	1 Kings 9:4

SUMMARY 5
DEVELOPING ACTS OF TRUST-INTEGRITY

Before starting this exercise, please read and follow the instruction in the preface of this workbook. Answers to these questions are contained in this chapter. Completion of these exercises after reading the chapter should take 60-90 minutes

Discovering the Acts of Trust-Integrity

1. What is the role of Trust-Integrity as an element of integrity?
2. Define integrity. What does the Bible teach about integrity?

3. How did the life of Jesus demonstrate acts of integrity? (Hebrew 4:15). (John 14:6). How you measure your work of integrity? (Philippians 4:8, ESV).
4. What important lesson can we learn from the life of Apostle Paul with respect to lige of integrity?.
5. What did Apostle Peter teach about life of integrity? (1 Peter 3:10-12, NKJV).
6. How did the following biblical leaders fail the test of integrity and never finished strong.?
   a. Adam, (Genesis 4);
   b. Abraham (Genesis 12); Genesis 16);
   c. David,(2 Samuel 11,12, 13);
   d. Moses (Numbers 20:7-11).

Practicing the acts of Trust-integrity

1. How can we Pursue a model life of integrity?
2. What does Apostle Paul imply when he said, "For we aim at what is honorable not only in the Lord's sight but also in the sight of man" (2 Corinthians 8:21, ESV)?.
3. Why did Apostle Paul focus on the training of the character of leaders like Timothy and Titus (1 Timothy 3:1–3; Titus 2:1–4; II Peter 3:14–15).
4. Authentic leaders live out a life of integrity by a code of conduct defined by 9 qualities. Name those qualities
5. Review the short list of characteristics of a person that can be considered to have integrity with wholeness and completeness in Table 5.1. How many of these 38 characteristics would you say you practice most frequently?

CHAPTER 6
DISPLAYING TRUST-CREDIBLITY

Credibility is the power to attract believability, trustworthiness, and authenticity to yourself; it is the believability, trustworthiness, and authenticity of who you are inside and outside. A leader cannot earn or receive trust without credibility. Building credibility starts at the personal level. A person's reputation is a direct reflection of his or her credibility, and it precedes them in any interactions or negotiations they might have. The four elements of credibility, according to Steve Covey, are integrity, intent, capability, and results. To begin developing self-leadership, a servant must check for these four elements and build these four cores of credibility at a personal level. Self-leadership is defined as "a process that occurs within an individual, rather than an external act." [63] It is an expression of who we are as people.

Set goals and communicate results

Accountable leaders set goals and communicate results to build credibility. People develop confidence and trust in a leader based on measuring what the leader has accomplished. What a leader has accomplished is measured relative to a set of goals and expectations. Like the State of the Union speech for a president, a leader must clearly define the levels of accountability in relation to goals and is then expected to be evaluated by how well he meets the objectives The expectation must be communicated patiently to all members of the organization. Starting with the leaders to the lowest person in the organization, a leader holds himself and every direct report responsible for consistently meeting the established and understood expectations. Credibility comes when people see and believe you accomplished what you said you would execute.

Gain others' confidence through credible associations

Leaders display confidence in others by associating with credible people. A measure of self-confidence of a good leader is his assuredness in his ability to achieve desired results or his self-assurance in his actions. For example, a leader's assuredness to keep his enemies close and his friends closer our self-confidence. Doris Kearns Goodwin, in her book, *Team of Rivals* gave an account of Lincoln's confidence in filling his cabinet posts. In defending his decision, Lincoln said: "I have looked the party over and concluded that these are the strongest men. Then I had no right to deprive the country of their service." [64] That was self-confidence! President Obama, who considers Lincoln his hero followed the same example in 2008 in selecting his cabinet. He said to ABC News' Sunlen Miller, "And, you know; one of my heroes is Abraham Lincoln. Lincoln appointed three of his rivals for the GOP presidential nomination to his cabinet. That has to be the approach that one takes whether it is choosing the vice president or the cabinet; whoever. By the way, that does not exclude Republicans either. You know my attitude is that whoever is the best person for the job is the person I want." [65] In the end, President Obama selected Senator Joe Biden as Vice President and Hillary Clinton as Secretary of State. This again is an act that can only come from a self-confident leader. Leaders can exemplify self-confidence in their ability to share power. Giving responsibility, authority, and control to various organizational members is an important statement of a leader's confidence in others and confidence in his judgment. It is also a way to extend trust to others.

Live outwardly from your inward

Be an inside-out leader to display credibility externally. Jesus Christ is addressing the crowd and His disciples on the subject of credibility and says; "For you are like whitewashed tombs, which indeed appear beautiful outwardly, but inside are full of dead men's bones and all uncleanness. Even so, you also outwardly appear righteous to men, but inside you are full of hypocrisy and lawlessness" (Matthew 23:23-30, NKJV).

Two important notes must be made here: First, Jesus was addressing one of the self-righteous attributes of servant leadership; that is, hypocrisy. Hypocrisy is the direct opposite of credibility. The Lord calls leader-servants to be inside-out leaders to reflect credibility. Second, the measuring stick of a leader-servant is Jesus Christ and who knows the inside all of us. We measure ourselves "Unto the measure of the status of the fullness of Christ" (Ephesians 4:13). The Apostle

Paul emphasized that what is most important is a change from the inside-out Leaders are to be inside-out Christians. "...but he is a Jew, who is one inwardly; and circumcision is that of the heart, in the Spirit, not in the letter; whose praise is not from men but from God" (Romans 2:28-29, NKJV).

God looks at our insides. When He wanted to select a leader to lead His people to Israel, He asked Samuel to anoint the king from Jesse's seed for the nation of Israel to succeed Saul. Samuel called Jesse's sons and began to examine them (I Samuel 16). What was he looking for? Without prior knowledge of these eight sons, and bearing in mind the need for a physically strong leader, one would look for a leader based on outward appearance.

How do you base your evaluation of yourself, a brand new manager, or a new youth director you want to hire? With what do you compare the qualities when you look at the CV? What is the basis of your measure? It is natural to compare ourselves or someone at some level with what we see and read. So it was that Samuel looked at Eliab and said, "Surely the Lord's anointed is before Him!" (I Samuel 16:6). The Lord looked at the inside and declared that Eliab was not qualified. God said to Samuel, "For the Lord does not see as a man sees; for man looks at the outward appearance, but the Lord looks at the heart" (1 Samuel 16: 7, NKJV). David, as the youngest of the eight sons, would be the least obvious choice for a leadership position in the eyes of the people; indeed, even a man of God like Samuel looked at the outside. However, God wanted a leader with a gentle and tender heart and yet someone who had an extremely courageous and very loving character, a man after His own heart. He saw that about the inside of David.

SERVANT LEADERSHIP TRANSFORMATIVE PRINCIPLES

How do we change inwardly so that our outside displays our credibility? Credibility is the power a leader has to attract believability, trustworthiness, and authenticity.
Let's consider the following credibility principles to build trust in transformative servant leadership:

Principle #1: Inward personal transformation yields external credibility

Our individual development is an internal process that builds the external credibility of a leader. One part of personal development is improving intrapersonal communication through self-reflective analysis alongside self-awareness. Leaders also build credibility by focusing on outward displays of inward attitudes, behaviors, and beliefs. These qualities can be developed through the habits of effective people and understanding how to lead from the inside out Kevin Cashman, in his book, *Leadership from the Inside Out*, defined leadership as an "authentic self-expression that creates value and discussed the seven pathways to lead from the inside." [66] Hackman and Johnson, in their book, *Leadership: A Communication Perspective* summarized these seven pathways as follows: [63]

Pathway 1: Personal Master. Pathway 1: Personal Master. This is a pathway of exploring who you are inside. Getting to know yourself and what is most important to you will impact your approach to leadership. Cashman suggests the following exploratory questions: What do I believe about myself and other people? What do I believe about leadership? What do I believe about life and the world?

Pathway 2: Purpose Mastery. This is a pathway that focuses on how you can cause a change in what you do. A good understanding of how can make a difference, using your gifts and talents will help you add value to those around you by identifying activities that are energizing and exciting.

Pathway 3: Change Mastery. This pathway focuses on being open-minded and disposed to change. This involves letting go of old, nonproductive, or nonessential patterns and developing new patterns to enhance creativity; being adaptable and willing to change; and changing current reality to see a fresh reality, such as going back to school to train in a fresh field.

Pathway 4: Interpersonal Mastery. This is a focus on building interpersonal relationships. Research has shown that middle and upper managers scored lowest in interpersonal skills compared to intellectual and technical skills. According to Cashman, focusing on developing interpersonal competencies and seeking feedback from others will help improve personal relationships.

Chapter 6
Displaying Trust-Credibility

Pathway 5: Being Mastery. Cashman defined "being" as an individual's core. He suggested that leaders could take time to find their inner strength of character and being by using periods of peace and silence such as quiet moments, listening to music, inspirational reading, and meditation.

Pathway 6: Balance Mastery. This concept relates to balancing one's life. Taking time for self, family, and friends is critical for maintaining balance in life. Achieving balance may be one of the most difficult pathways to master, but is the most important; balancing one's life (work, personal, relationships, family, etc.) is a long-time process because it is dynamic and always changing.

Pathway 7: Action Mastery. This concept includes learning to lead as a whole person by getting in touch with one's authentic self and expressing it to others. It is about being you.

Principle #2: Transforming your mind-power changes your credibility.

The most corrupting driver of your inside is your thoughts and desires. Transforming your mind begins by bringing your thoughts into obedience to Christ's teaching and building your power to transform others. Here are key actions you can take to transform your thoughts:

Control and channel your thoughts to your positive purposeful growth. A positive growth purpose is one that is in line with A positive growth purpose is one that is in line with the perfect will of God for you. Paul writes, *"Be not conformed to this world; but be ye transformed by the renewing of your mind, so that ye may prove what is that good, and acceptable, and perfect, will of God" (Romans 12:1-3).* Your purpose in anything you do must be valid, admissible, and impeccable in God's plan for you. Being good alone is not sufficient even in your organization. If perfection is possible in whatever you do, then your purpose is merely adequate to a standard that is not enough, it does not meet standards. You must be above the world's standard. That implies creating a culture of excellence that transforms followers' minds toward excellence. To begin to transform your mind, you are called to humility; your thoughts are not to make you think of yourself more highly than you ought to think. Your action is not to be conformed to those of the world's standard but the excellence of the standard of God's perfection. As a leader, you must work to transform your mind by renewing it daily and bringing it in line with the positive purpose and will of God. Your everyday beneficial attitude changes your inside to bear the fruit that transforms your outward conduct, such as integrity, credibility, and motives. Your mind is also transformed to excellence to the level of the new information and knowledge you are able to gain or add to your mind.

Cast down all imaginations that are not aligned with God's Word or your positive purposeful growth plan. Imagination and fantasizing can simply be such things as entertaining negative thoughts, imagining bad plans, or any thought contrary to the word of God. Imaginations also include not forgetting the past but dwelling on it and trying to figure it out for ourselves. Imaginations are playing out thoughts beyond our external control. To be a leader with positive outward dispositions, these imaginations must be cleaned out, captured, and transformed into thoughts aligned with the Word of God (2 Corinthians 10:5-6) or your purposeful growth plan Our thoughts are crucial because they are the first link in the chain reaction that defiles our inside. We must bring our prideful imagination into captivity (under our control) after casting down (rejecting) such damaging thoughts. Our thoughts stir up our emotions; our emotions then influence our desires; and our desires produce our actions. Our actions, good or bad, create our habits and attitudes, and our habits and attitudes develop our character, whether it is good or bad. Taking every bad thought captive will prevent that chain reaction before it even begins. Anything that exalts itself has the tendency to stir up pride and defile our humility to serve.

Our humility is one cure for worldliness and poor attitude to service. Thus, we must reject pride in all of its forms. The Scripture says, "God resists the proud…But gives grace to the humble. Therefore submit to God… Humble yourselves in the sight of the Lord, and He will lift you up" (James 4:6-10, NKJV). To become an inside-out leader means we must be humble and gentle in spirit.

Examine your thoughts through the Holy Spirit in us (1 John 4:1-2) God's (good) thoughts or God's promptings come through that still small voice that immediately bears witness with our spirit, which is, indeed, God's voice. God's voice encourages us and draws us closer to Him. The health of our insides is seen by the Holy Spirit, who bears witness to our spirit (our mind), that we are the children of God

(Romans 8:16). The human spirit is that part of a man who knows the intellect, mind, and will. God's voice is always going to be in perfect agreement with His written Word. "There is no condemnation to them that are in Christ Jesus, who walk not after the flesh but after the Spirit" (Romans 8:1). To be an inside-out leader, we must weed out spurious thoughts that defile us. Be able to test all spirits, whether they are from God. The scripture says; "Every spirit that acknowledges that Jesus Christ has come in the flesh is from God" (4: 2, ESV).

Bad thoughts (those not from God) come from two other sources: the flesh and Devil. Our negative thoughts that are not led by the Spirit would be "things of the flesh," that is, anything that is not of the Spirit. These are self-centered things that need to be immediately confessed (especially if we have held on to them for any length of time), repent, and given over to God. With these actions, the Devil will not be able to use them to bring us down. "For the weapons of our warfare are not carnal, but mighty through God to the pulling down of strongholds" (2 Corinthians 10:3-4). Devil's voice is very different from God's; He speaks to us in a loud, shrill, and demanding voice full of deceit. It's urgent, "do it now" kind of thought, and it often prompts unrest and doubt. Devil uses all sorts of tactics to condemn us and make us feel guilty. He likes failures in Christians. These kinds of thoughts come from Devil or his tool to weaken our faith.

Understand your power, authority, and identity. There are many confusing definitions of power and authority in the literature. Some define the two as the same and can be used interchangeably. I believe there are differences. Let us use our police officer analogy again. When you see a police officer well dressed in the usual police gear, besides all things you can see on him, and depending on the assignment or department of that officer, you will notice three essential elements: a badge or symbol (seal of authority), some weapon (implied approval to use it), and a name identity tag (the person). All three elements are visibly displayed for one reason: to show that this *person* is an *authority* of the law (local, state, and federal) and has the *power* to use that authority. Thus, a police officer has the legitimate authority to arrest an offender of the law. Pilate thought he had the power to crucify Jesus, but in reality, he had no authority. Pilate said to Him, "Are You not speaking to me? Do You not know that I have the power to crucify You, and the power to release You? And Jesus answered,

"You could have no power at all against Me unless it had been given you from above" [John 19:10-11, NKJV). Jesus' emphasis could be, "you think you have power but that power is powerless over me because you have no authority over me."

So what is the difference between authority and power? Authority is given to someone to exercise power over another or something. So a thief may have the power to break in to steal but he has no authority given by anybody. Here are two definitions:

Power is the ability or capacity to force or influence the law; your will, or your actions on others because of your position or might. The primary sources of power base are the knowledge you possess, your position, your identity, authority, and others. Terry R. Bacon (2011) in his book, *The Elements of Power: Lessons on Leadership and Influence*, listed the eleven sources of power which include the following: five *personal sources* (knowledge, expressiveness, history [familiarity], attraction, and character), five *organizational sources* (role, resources, information, network, and reputation), and one *meta-source*, will).[67]

Authority is the right given to someone to do something, willingly or unwilling because of the giver's positional influence or right given to influence others to get desired action toward a goal. So in this regard, authority often comes from whom you are, your leadership positional responsibilities, and what you are. Authority is one source of power a leader has. Without authority, power becomes powerless. For example, a police officer without an arrest warrant as an example of authority cannot arrest a criminal. On the hand, without power, authority becomes ineffective to influence a desired change in people. So both are different but related!

Understand Devil's key tactics to deceive your mind to defile your credibility. This is an important strategy to consider if we must be successful in transforming our thoughts to build credibility. Some of the Devil's principal tactics come from Genesis 3 where he used the serpent as his tool and from Matthew 4 in his bold temptation of Jesus. In Genesis 3:1-5, the Devil's main three deceptive tactics to cause the original fall of man were:

- **Deception to Doubt our Beliefs.** The serpent as Devil's tool deceitfully misquoted God's word from Gen 2:16-17 and used man's desires to excite the natural curiosity and doubt about the purpose and truth of God's Word (3.1). The woman's addition,

"nor shall you touch it" was not even part of God's command in Genesis 2:16-17, showing that Devil was succeeding in his plan to confuse the actual communication God had with Adam.
- **Deception to Discount God** by Contradiction. By deception and misinterpretation of the Word of God, Devil gave a man false hope by knowingly ignoring, contradicting, or discounting the judgment of God for disobedience to His Word. "You will not surely die" (Genesis 3.4). This is contrary to what God had commanded earlier, "The day that you eat of it; you shall surely die" (Genesis 2: 17b). Devil's purpose was mainly to plant doubt as to the execution of the penalty for disobedience.
- **Deception to Defame God's Character.** The devil's tactic here was to defame God by making God a liar and questioning the trustworthiness and truthfulness of the character of God; his purpose was to incite man to see God as a liar and to doubt if God really loves him (Genesis 3.5).

Devil played a mind game with Eve in the above account, and we must be aware of this type of manipulation from the devil to build transformative credibility. Sadly, Eve was both ill-informed and emotionally too weak to resist him; she unduly believed the Devil. The result was that man yielded to Devil's trap and transgressed against God. "So when the woman saw that the tree was good for food (desire), that it was pleasant to the eyes (lust), and a tree desirable to make one wise (power), she took of its fruit and ate" (Genesis 3:6, NKJV). We see the same pattern of the Devil's cunningness today in leadership. Devil made Eve see this tree with a different worldly mind-eye and created doubt and curiosity as to what God said. The antidote to such tactics is to live and walk in the Spirit (Galatian 5:25). Living and walking in the Spirit means being vigilant with readiness to test our thoughts through the Word of God and the Holy Spirit in us. God directly communicated the message and command to Adam even before Eve was created. Adam lost his credibility as the first leader-servant because he;

(1) *Faulty communication*: He failed in his role because of faulty communication with his wife Eve

(2) *Details Ignored.* He Ignored some details of the communication God gave to him alone.

(3) *Wrong Influence*: He allowed Eve's emotions, desires, and voice to influence him more than God's voice,

(4) *No accountability:* He failed to hold himself accountable for not preserving the correct message God entrusted to him,

(5) *Consequences for disobedience ignored*: He disregarded what God had commanded as a consequence if he disobeyed,

(6) *No Responsibility*: He failed to take responsibility for the results of his disobedience to God's command.

The result: Adam lost credibility with God, Man, and Devil, but gained death for himself and humanity. Adam allowed Eve's voice to cloud his thinking and ability to make the right judgment; he failed to understand the full message that God communicated to him. Adam failed in every test of accountability because he ceased to take responsibility for his failure. Devil knew and saw Adam's vulnerability and used it to bring to his fall. God was very specific in His communication with Adam, but he allowed the negative influence of his wife to weaken his resistance.

For Eve, understand where Eve failed:

(1) She usurped the authority of her husband (by not consulting with him,

(2) She was influenced by her desire and emotions; and

(3) Allowed herself to be deceived and so transgressed God's law and in turn deceived her husband.

The result; is "her desire shall be for her husband, and he shall rule over you" (Genesis 3:16 see also I Timothy 2:12-14). One may wonder why Devil went to Eve rather than Adam. It could be because Devil knew that Eve was the weaker one emotionally and love beautiful things more; he knew that Eve was not there when the communication was given, and therefore was more likely to be confused; he also knew that if he could get the wife, it was possible he could get the husband through the wife. Devil used Eve as the ultimate tool to bring Adam down. The leaders are responsible for their success or failure and should be vigilant to know that their success or failure could depend on their closest associations, such as their wives or husbands.

There are three very essential elements of communication: concentrating, hearing, and understanding. Effective communication fails if any of these fails or is faulty. In which of these did Adam fail? Adam heard God because he was concentrating. Adam's major failure was in belie understanding all aspects of what God commanded. Understand and use your identity as a source of the power of authority to guard your thoughts. One source of power as stated above that a leader has is the information he has coupled with his identity and authority to use that information. This can be illustrated through the account of Devil's temptation of Jesus, and His response based on His identity and the power He has compared to that of Adam, and Eve described above. In Matthew, 4:2-10 Devil's three main tactics were:

(1) **False use of power to meet human needs.** Jesus was hungry and needed sustenance after 40 days and 40 nights of fasting in the desert. The devil used this occasion to present his path for self-sufficiency; "If You are the Son of God, command that these stones become bread" (Matthew 4:2-4). Yes, Jesus was the Son of God. The natural inclination for today's leaders would be to show that he was and had the power. However, Jesus was ahead of the devil. He knew his main purpose and wanted to show the devil that God is all-sufficiency. He said, "It is written, 'Man shall not live by bread alone, but by every word that proceeds from the mouth of God."

(2) **False use of power for fame ((Matthew 4:5-7).** There is no limit to which the devil can go in deceiving a leader. And truly, men of God today continue to commit spiritual or sometimes physical suicide, as the devil was attempting to do here, by ignoring the trap of the enemy. The devil knew that his kingdom is doomed to fail if he could destroy who Jesus was as early as possible. So he said; "If You are the Son of God, throw Yourself down. For it is written: 'He shall give His angels charge over you'" (Matthew 4:6). This once again is the devil's intentional misquote from Psalm 91:11-12, just to deceive. Jesus was ahead of him, and quoted from Deuteronomy 6:16, "It is written again, 'You shall not tempt the LORD your God.'" (Matthew 4:7, NKJV). He was saying to Satan that His power was not for His fame or self-promotion. Meaning, "Look Devil, I know your plot"; "I know you have come to steal, to kill and to destroy" (John 10.10). Jesus was clearly telling him 'I am smarter than you; I know you are trying to tempt me." This

must be the type of transforming thought of a leader who must finish strong!

(3) Easy path for power and glory (Matthew 4:8-10). Power and glory are two great values of secular leadership. Satan after showing Jesus a glimpse of the glory, could get presents his simple shortcut to gain these, "All these things I will give You if You will fall down and worship me." The devil cannot give to Jesus what is His in the first place; "The earth is the LORD's, and everything in it, the world, and all who live in it" (Psalm 24.1, NIV). In the devil's third temptation, Jesus was more resolute and with righteous indignation rebuked and commanded him saying, "Away with you, Satan! For it is written, 'You shall worship the LORD your God, and Him only you shall serve.'" (Matthew 4:10, NKJV).

In the above encounter with the devil, what was Jesus' key weapon against him? What about Adam and Eve, what were their weapons? Jesus's key weapons were His power, authority, and identity. His rebuke to the devil was an intense command based on His power, "Away with you, Satan" or "Away from me, Satan." Some version renders it "Be gone, Satan" (Matthew 4: 10, ESV). Jesus also quoted from the Old Testament (Deuteronomy 6:13, Isaiah 9: 1-2) but with authority. His use of "it is written" was to show that He is the fulfillment of the Old Testament scriptures. Unlike in the case of Adam and Eve, Jesus resisted the devil and was each time ahead of him. The result was that the devil left Him, while the angels came and ministered to Him. Jesus knew His identity as the Son of God and that the devil cannot give Him the power He already has and knew that only His Father is worthy of worship. Sadly, Adam did not have any winning strategy; he delegated his responsibility to Eve. What a contrast between the two responses! We must as leaders recognize that we are in a mind battle, and whoever controls our thinking will ultimately control our lives, even our destinies. We will win the battle if we just know the attitudes and essential steps for renewing our minds and understanding the devices of the enemy to deceive us.

Have you ever been stopped by or seen a police officer in full uniform with offensive and defensive gear? No matter, the stature of the officer, he or she usually appears with power and authority and knows how to use them. A police officer once stopped for a traffic violation. As row down my window and wanted to ask for forgiveness, he said, "Keep quiet sir. Before I stopped you, I was ready to write you a citation." He was stern in his voice and told me, "Look; I am not your friend. I am the law." The officer is backed by the state or city laws and is ready, without intimidation or hesitation, to use the power if necessary to arrest an offender or any impending danger. So we must be leader-servants. We have been clothed with a garment of righteousness and the mighty power of God to pull down strongholds and negative imaginations originating from the deceptive thoughts of the devil. Power means nothing unless we use it. Otherwise, the work of God suffers and the devil wins. Unless we stand with indignation against the devil and whatever tools he uses, we will continue to be his to manipulate and enslave. If you do not know who you are or what you have, the devil will tell you who you are and give you what he has. The devil that Jesus called; *"a liar and the father of all lies"* (John 8:44, NIV) has no credibility and must not be trusted if you must build true credibility that transforms others.

Present your body as living sacrifices, holy and acceptable to God (Romans 12:1). What does this scripture mean? We are to bring ourselves (living sacrifices) to God instead of (dead) sacrifices (as of old). These are sacrifices performed with the heart, mind, and soul of intelligent beings rather than the idols of old. Every day, we must give God permission to walk through us and expose anything in us that is "not of faith." We must willingly offer ourselves to Him for His examination. This means that we must be willing, daily, to allow His Holy Spirit to search us and expose whatever He wants in each of us. David said, "Search me, O God, and know my heart: try me, and know my thoughts: And see if there be any wicked way in me, and lead me in the way everlasting" (Psalms 139:23-24).

Deny ourselves whatever (thoughts, emotions, and desires) is contrary to what He desires. The attitude of denying ourselves concerns transforming our "inner man" and setting aside our thoughts, emotions, and desires—our self-life—so that God can fill us with His Life. How can we do this? "If any man will come after Me [Jesus], let him deny himself, and take up his cross, and follow Me" (Matthew 16:24). This means we must be willing to set aside all of our self-centered ways, our rights, our frustrations, offenses, even our expectations, comparisons, and presumptions and follow God's ways in faith. Luke 14:26 reminds us that we cannot be God's disciples unless we are agreeable to (not just wanting to or feeling like it) to lay everything down. In Jesus' words, "If anyone comes to Me and does not hate his father and mother, wife and children, brothers and sisters, yes, and his own life also, he cannot be My disciple" (Luke 4:26, NIV)

Obey God's will: Be desirous to get up and do exactly what He asks you to do. This attitude calls for being disposed to do what God has asked us to do. No matter what our thoughts or feelings are, no matter what we think or what we want, we must be willing to do exactly what God has asked here; "As there was a readiness to will [or to choose], so there may be a performance [doing in action]." 2 Corinthians 8:11. The attitude concerns the transformation of our outward actions toward God. We are emotional creatures, and God is asking us to set aside our own sentimental responses and choose to act totally out of faith. That comes from an inside-out attitude that means completely surrendering to God. Can you imagine how Abraham's faith must have increased when he obeyed God? (Genesis 22:1-14)? The first action of a transformed mind knows what is; the "good, acceptable and perfect will of God"(Romans 12:2, NIV). We are then able to believe in God, and our faith comes from our transformed mind as it hears the Word of God. Faith is the shield with which we overcome the world (1 John 5), and it is strengthened continuously by regeneration from the Holy Spirit.

Principle #3: Self-assessment of our inward parts positions our credibility

In addition to our thoughts that defile our internal man, sin is the greatest culprit and must be kept in check by examining our lives daily and continuously to reveal and deal with the root of sin in our lives. Sin originates from our behaviors, desires, lack of forgiveness, or any behavior that appears to control us and compromise our inner man. For any organization, this means dealing with unresolved issues that create relationship and communication walls between you and your followers, your circle of influence, and those to whom you report. How do we look into our character to prevent wrongful or unacceptable behaviors? Or why do some leaders, even church leaders, engage in sinful behavior? Finding the answer could be the beginning of needed healing.

Partnership with God sustains credibility. The apex of a leadership pyramid can often be lonely for some leaders. Christian leaders' paths can also be challenging in a world that is becoming ever more godless. Christians are constantly battling against the unrighteousness in this world and personal sins in their lives. We read of some women of God, who to get a job for which they were very qualified or a merited promotion had to contend with sexual advances from their boss. Pastors and reputable ministers struggle to manage, in the words of Pastor Mike Milley of White Dove Fellowship, Harvey LA, the "Three Gs: the Girls, the Glory, and the Goodies." Leaders who seek to be transformed inside-out must be persistent in purity. Paul wrote; "Therefore, we do not lose heart. Even though our outward man is perishing, yet the inward man is being renewed day by day."2 Corinthians 4:16. We need to be persistent in resisting sin and fighting the battle to stay pure inside. The devil's target is to steal our hearts from God, kill our fellowship with God, and defile our insides. Servant Leaders need to be incessant in renewing their inward man to become credible inside-out leaders. We can be only persistent in renewing our internal man through a partnership with God through His Word and the Holy Spirit to guard our hearts toward purity and holiness.

A Case of Credibility: David after God's Heart

A Case Study of Credibility: David after God's Heart illustrates this principle #3: Leader-Servants need to be persistent in renewing their inward man to become credible inside-out leaders. David was a king described as a man after God's heart, but he sinned against God. What did David do to get healing?

Elements of David's Prayer

In Psalm 51:1-19 (NKJV), we read David's sincere self-examination of his character and actions when he repented for the sins he had committed. We can study David's prayer under the following five critical elements: repentance, responsibility, renewal, restoration, and restitution:

Repentance and forgiveness are requested: "Have mercy upon me...Blot out my transgressions...Wash me thoroughly from my iniquity; cleanse me from my sin; I acknowledge my transgressions; my sin is always before me" (Psalm 51: 1-2, NKJV)

Responsibility acknowledged: David acknowledged that his sins were against God: "Against You, You only, have I sinned." He also acknowledges that there are consequences for his sins; "You may be found just when You speak, and blameless when You judge" (Psalm 51: 3-4, NKJV)

Renewal, purging, and cleansing requested: David self-examined his inward man and he needed cleansing. He said, 'I was brought forth in iniquity, And in sin, my mother conceived me". He knew he was responsible for what he had done; He knew that God desires truth in the inward parts of his heart; David asked for wisdom because he has been compromised by sin and he needed renewal from the inside out; he asked God to purge him to make him clean. "Wash me, and I shall be whiter than snow" (Psalm 51:5-7)

Restoration requested: He requested restored joy and gladness that had broken him down physically; he requested that his iniquities be blotted out and for God to create in him a clean heart and to renew a steadfast spirit within him; Most importantly, David desired God to restore His presence, Holy Spirit; the joy of His salvation, and His generous Spirit. (Psalm 51:8-12). To David, the joy of the Lord is the main source of his inward man which displays credibility before God and is seen by his followers outside.

Restitution committed to God: David in this last part made a commitment to use his "ashes" and experiences to bless others and to glorify God; to teach transgressors God's ways, use his tongue and mouth to sing aloud of God's righteousness and show forth God's praise; He will gladly offer sacrifices from a crushed spirit, a broken and contrite heart, and of righteousness to God (Psalm 51:13-19). These commitments in David's prayer are very significant. They were designed as offers of his sacrifices and restitution to regain trust and credibility in God, who earlier had, testified of David: "I have found David, the son of Jesse, a man after My own heart, who will do all My will" (Acts 12:22; cp: 1 Samuel 13:14). God honored David's request and never removed him as King until his death.

What mattered most to David

Looking at the above five elements of David's prayer, what exactly was the most important thing to David: Was David repentant because he was caught in the act or because, deep down, in him; he wanted to restore his fellowship with God? I believe it was the latter than the former. David desired the following three interdependent things from God purposely to renew his inward brokenness and broken fellowship with God. At this point, in David's struggles with this sin, he hated what he felt inside of him; he was so miserable that nothing mattered but to regaining credibility before God.

David desired complete purging and cleansing to look pure before God. David looked deep into his soul and what he saw was a filth that needed to be purged and cleaned to be "whiter than snow." He wanted God to remove all traces of the filth and the roots of the sin that defiled his inside. Our transformation from the inside out must therefore begin with a self-awareness that we are filthy and need cleansing. This attitude change begins from our innermost part and proceeds outwardly to change our behavior and hence our credibility as leaders.

David desired the restoration of the violated fellowship. Restoration of the broken fellowship with God begins with self-examination and accepting the responsibility for the sin. David acknowledged without mixing words that God wanted truth and wisdom in his inward parts but that his inside has been made filthy by his transgression. The result was that the filth inside stained his outside, the external pillars that supported his credibility. Most important to David was the fact the filth strained his fellowship with God and the joy of salvation. Outwardly, King David was a great and powerful King, but inwardly he was an adulterer, a murderer, and a deceiver. David felts that a defiled inward man cannot display credible fellowship with God.

David desired inside-out transformation for renewed fellowship with God. Inside-out renewed fellowship with God is what is required, not only to repair but sustain the broken fellowship. Inwardly, and even with his transgression, David was a man after God's own heart, and fellowship with God was very important to him. It is no surprise that David's main focus was on an inside-out, top-down transformation, a new clean heart, a renewed fellowship with God, continued empowerment by the Holy Spirit, and a restoration of the joy of his salvation.

David could be remembered by man for his sins and deceptions to cover them, but in God's heart, David was a king with a contrite heart that desired restoration to his relationship with God more than any man that ever lived. And God honored him!

The Apostle Paul recognized the need for this purging while acknowledging his inward struggles with sin: "So I find this law at work: Although I want to do good, evil is right there with me" (Romans 7:21, NIV). To be inside-out leader-servants, we need to have and delight in God's law in our inward being (Romans 7:22). This will empower us not only to live in the Spirit but also to walk in the Spirit (Galatians 5:25) as a critical attitude for complete purging and sustained cleaning.

SUMMARY 6
DEVELOPING THE ACTS OF TRUST-CREDIBILITY

Before starting this exercise, please read and follow the instruction in the preface of this workbook. Answers to these questions are contained in this chapter. Completion of these exercises after reading the chapter should take 60-90 minutes.

Discovering the Acts of Trust-Credibility

1. What is Credibility?
2. Can one earn or receive trust without credibility?.
3. What are the four elements of credibility, according to Steve Covey, are integrity, intent, capability, and results [63]?
4. How is credibility is the power a leader must have to attract believability, trustworthiness, and authenticity.?

Practicing the Acts of Trust-Credibility

1. How do Accountable leaders set goals and communicate results to build credibility?
2. How can a leader gain others' confidence through credible associations

3. Jesus Christ in addressing the crowd and His disciples on the subject of credibility said, "For you are like whitewashed tombs, which indeed appear beautiful outwardly, but inside are full of dead men's bones and all uncleanness. Even so, you also outwardly appear righteous to men, but inside you are full of hypocrisy and lawlessness" (Matthew 23:23-30, NKJV).
    a. What two points was Jesus making here? (see also Romans 2:28-29, NKJV).
4. When God wanted to select a leader to lead His people to Israel, He asked Samuel to anoint the king from Jesse's seed for the nation of Israel to succeed Saul. Compare what God was looking for to what Prophet Samuel looked for in the selection (I Samuel 16).
5. How do you base your evaluation of yourself and others in the different situations you encounter?

Understanding Trust Credibility Leadership Transformative Principles

1. Let's consider the following credibility principles to build trust in transformative servant leadership:
2. ***Principle #1: Inward personal transformation yields external credibility.*** How do we change inwardly so that our outside displays our credibility?
    a. What do I believe about myself and other people? What do I believe about life and the world?
    b. **How can be** open-minded and disposed to change. How do you build interpersonal relationships.
    c. How can you find your inner strength of character?
    d. How do you achieve balance in life (work, personal, relationships, family, etc.).
    e. **How do you** learning to lead as a whole person

3. ***Principle #2: Transforming your mind-power changes your credibility.*** The most corrupting driver of your inside is your thoughts and desires.
    a. How do transform your mind for positive purpose?
    b. What is the difference between Power and authority ? How Power corrupting? List The Elements of Power[67]

    c. In Genesis 3:1-6, what are three deceptive tactics of the Devil's to cause the original fall of man
    d. How and why did Adam lose his credibility as the first leader-servant?
    e. What was the result of Adam losing credibility
    f. Where and how did Eve fail? What was the result?
    g. In Matthew, 4:2-10 what were the Devil's three main tactics against Jesus?
    h. In the above encounter with the devil, what was Jesus' key weapon against him? What about Adam and Eve, what were their weapons?

Practicing acts of Trust -Credibility: A Case of Credibility of David after God's Heart

1. A Case Study of Credibility: David after God's Heart illustrates this principle #3: Leader-Servants need to be persistent in renewing their inward man to become credible inside-out leaders. David was a king described as a man after God's heart, but he sinned against God. In Psalm 51:1-19)
    a. What did David do to get healing?
    b. What were the Elements of David's Prayer as he sincerely self-examined himself?
    c. What mattered most to David?
    d. Looking at the five elements of David's prayer, what exactly was the most important thing to David: Was David repentant because he was caught in the act or because, deep down, in him; he wanted to restore his fellowship with God?
2. The Apostle Paul recognized the need for this purging while acknowledging his inward struggles with sin: "So I find this law at work: Although I want to do good, evil is right there with me" (Romans 7:21, NIV).
    a. What is Paul saying you need to be inside-out leader-servant (Romans 7:22; Galatians 5:25)

Topic Index

About This Book, 24
Affective Compassion, 73
authentic, 26, 28, 86
authentic leadership, 39
Authentic Leadership, 47
Authenticity, 45
Characteristics of Servant Leadership
   Trust Attribute, 58
Characteristics of Leadership
   Servanthood Attribute, 54
Comfort, 43
commitment, 21, 27
Comparisons
   with other works, 42
credibility, 50
Credibility, 84
Credibility Principle
   Personal Transformation, 86, 104
Discipleship
   definition of, 29
distinguishes
   a leader's act of giving, 31
diversity, 63
Elements of David's Prayer
   what mattered most to David, 101, 105
Functional Definitions, 37
Generosity
   definition of, 31
Generosity c, 31
giving, 31
   habit of, 31
humility, 89
imaginations
   casting down, 88
inside-out, 48, 84, 89
Integrity
   code of conduct, 76, 80
   life of, 73

   model of, 74, 80
   pattern of truth., 74
   wholeness and trust, 75
John Maxwell, 67
Joshua, 21
law of, 44
Leader as Servant Leadership, 44
   definition, 27
Leader First., 25
Leader-as-Servant Leadership, 25
leader-servant's affection-attribute
   definition, 50
leadership, **27**
Leadership Attributes, 45
Leadership Inner Value system, 27
Model, 25
Moses, 21
Navigation-attribute, 50
Organizational leadership trust, 34, 54
Personal Master, 86
Personal Outward Authenticity, 49
power, authority
   defined and differentiated, 90
process, 27
relational connection, 54
Servant, 25, 26
tactics
   devils to deceive, 91
Teachable Moments to Grow, 80
test
   for leader-servant authenticity, 48
   of essential elements of personal
     authenticity, 48, 49
The Leadership Influence-attribute, 43
Trust, 55, 58, 61, 64, 67
trust attitude
   build commitment, 67

REFERENCES

[1]Greenleaf, R. (1970). *The Servant as Leader,* Indianapolis: The Robert K. Greenleaf Center

[2]Spears, L. (1996*).* "*Reflections on Robert K. Greenleaf and servant-leadership."* Leadership & Organization Development Journal, 17(7), 33-35

[3]Russell, R.F. (2001). "The role of values in servant leadership." *Leadership & Organization Development Journal,* 22(2), 76-83

[4]Russell, R.F., and Stone, A.G. (2002). "A review of servant leadership attributes: developing a practical model." *Leadership & Organization Development Journal,* 23(3), 145-15

[5]Terry. R. W (1993*). Authentic Leadership: Courage In Action,* San Francisco, CA ,Jossey-Bass

[6]George, B (2003). *Authentic Leadership: Rediscovering the Secrets to Creating Lasting Value.* San Francisco, CA, Jossey-Bass

[7]Shamir, B. & Eilam, G. (2005). "What's your story? Toward a life-story approach to authentic leadership." Leadership Quarterly, 16, 395–418.

[8]Anderson, GL (2009). Advocacy Leadership: Toward a Post-Reform Agenda in Education, Routledge, New York, 41

[9]Yacobi, B.G. *"Elements of Human Authenticity."* http://www.philosophytogo.org /wordpress/?p=1945, Retrieved, July 15, 2012

[10]George, B (2003). *Authentic Leadership: Rediscovering the Secrets to Creating Lasting Value,* San Francisco, CA, Jossey-Bass

[11]Wosu, SN (2014), *Leader as Servant Leadership Model,* Xulon Press

[12]Nee, Watchman (1988). *The Character of God's Workman,* Christian Fellowship Publisher, NY

[13]Slamka, S (2010). "Humility as a Catalyst for Compassion The Humility-Compassion Cycle of Helping Relevance to Counseling." College of St. Joseph In Vermont

http://compassionspace.com/sg_userfiles/revised_humility-compassion.pdf], Retrieved, July 2012

[14]Collins, Jim (2001). *Good to Great: Why Some Companies Make the Leap... and Others Don't* , Harper Business

[15]Warren, R (2002) *The Purpose Driven Life,* Published by Zondervan.

[16]King, Martin L, Jr. *The Strength of Love,* Pocket Books, 1964, p. 69).

[17]Stevenson, Mary. "*Footprints in the Sand.*" http://www.footprints-in-the-sand.com/index.php?page=Poem/Poem.php.

[18]Nelson Mandela (1994). *Long walk to Freedom,* Little, Brown and Company, New York

[19]Wosu, SN (2014). *Leader as Servant Leadership Model,* Xulon Press,

[53]Nelson Mandela (1994). *Long walk to Freedom,* Little, Brown and Company, New York.

[54]Wosu, SN (2014). *Leader as Servant Leadership Model,* Xulon Press,

[55]Lamb, L. F., McKee, K. B. (2004).*Applied Public Relations: Cases in Stakeholder Management.* Mahwah, New Jersey: Lawrence Erlbaum Associates. Routledge

[56]The Kenexa High Performance Institute (2011), WorkTrends

[57]Robbins, S (2005). *Organizational Behavior,* 11ed, Prentice Hall, Inc.

[58]Covey, S. (2004). *The Seven Habits of Highly Effective People.* New York, NY: Free Press, 47

[59]Lencioni, P (202). *The Five Dysfunctions of a Team*, San Francisco: Jossey-Bass, 43.

[60]Choung, J (2005). "Survey of Biblical Leaders" 9258A Regents Road. La Jolla, CA 92037. Retrieved Feb 5, 2014, http://cms.intervarsity.org/mx/item/4335/download/

[61]U.S. Army Handbook (1973). *Military Leadership*

[62]*Houdmann, S. M.* "What does the Bible say about integrity?" http://www.gotquestions.org/Bible-integrity.html.

REFERENCES

[63]Hackman, M. & Johnson, C. (2009). *Leadership: A communication perspective*. Long rove, IL: Waveland Press, Inc.

[64]Doris Kearns Goodwin (2005). Team of Rivals: Political Genius of Abraham L Lincoln, published Simon & Schuster

[65]ABC News' Sunlen Miller

[66]Cashman, K (2008). *Leadership from the Inside Out: Becoming a Leader for Life*, Berrett-Koehler, 2008

[67]Bacon, T.R (2011). "The Elements of Power: Lessons on Leadership and Influence" AMACOM Div American Mgmt Assn.

www.ingramcontent.com/pod-product-compliance
Lightning Source LLC
LaVergne TN
LVHW061555070526
838199LV00077B/7064